A CARNIVAL FILMS / MASTERPIECE CO-PRODUCTION

The CHRONICLES *of* DOWNTON ABBEY

FOREWORD
JULIAN FELLOWES

TEXT
JESSICA FELLOWES AND MATTHEW STURGIS

PHOTOGRAPHY
JOSS BARRATT, NICK BRIGGS
AND GILES KEYTE

ST. MARTIN'S PRESS

Violet

No family is ever
what it seems from
the outside

CONTENTS

JULIAN FELLOWES

FOREWORD

Over the last two rather extraordinary years, at the risk of sounding vain, I have often been asked why I thought *Downton Abbey* has been quite such a success. Of course it is hard to be definite about these things. If television were an exact science, there would be nothing made that did not break records. But supposing I were to put my finger on one element, it might be that we have made the decision to treat every character, the members of the family and the members of their staff, equally, in terms of their narrative strength. They all have emotional lives, dreams, ambitions and disappointments, and with all of them we suggest a back story. So this book, which is an invitation to get to know the characters and their backgrounds more fully, will, I hope, build on that and allow the reader to develop his or her relationship with the figures in our landscape.

In a way, the decision to write the show at all came out of emotional, rather than historical, curiosity. When Gareth Neame made the original suggestion that we should together travel back into *Gosford Park* land, this time for television, I was initially undecided, but it so happened that I was reading a book, *To Marry an English Lord*, which was about the Buccaneers – those American heiresses who arrived in such numbers during the 1880s and 90s, to rescue many great houses in distress. It occurred to me that while people had a mental image of beauties like Consuelo Vanderbilt or Cornelia Bradley-Martin stepping ashore into the (not always very willing) arms of a waiting nobleman, few bothered to think about those same women, 20, 30, 40 years later, marooned in some freezing country house in the Midlands, with envious thoughts of their sisters in their comfortable, centrally heated cottages in Newport. Most of them outlived the way of life they had arrived to save, dying in the 1950s and 60s, having devoted the years to a social and political system that the century finally rejected. How did they deal with that? It is not surprising that such ruminations led to more thinking and more characters, until I had made the decision to take on the job and the series was born. So, you could say Cora Grantham was the mother of *Downton Abbey*, which is no doubt just as it should be.

Few people shake off the family influences they were born into, and I am not among them. My relations, when I was young, were numerous and omnipresent and, inevitably I suppose, they seem now to abandon their graves and settle into the pages of my scripts with increasing regularity. I have spoken before of my impressive, if tyrannical, great-aunt, Isie, who is the principal model for Violet Grantham (and also for Lady Trentham in *Gosford Park*, before that), a woman whose dry wit concealed a good deal of personal suffering and who was no tougher on the rest of us than she was on herself. It is perhaps that draconian sense of personal discipline that makes her breed seem admirable to me. But my family has contributed the outline sketches for more than the Dowager. Robert Grantham is definitely drawn, in his personality if not his circumstance, from my dear departed father. In this, I mean to convey that he was a deeply moral man, cleverer possibly than Robert, who was always determined to do right, but without ever contesting the structure of his own social universe. One of my brothers remarked that if Pa had crashed in the desert and somehow found a parking meter buried in the sand, he would be sure to put the correct money into it. This stuff dies hard in us and not long ago, when I discovered I had taken change for a 20 pound note instead of a tenner from the branch of Tesco in Trafalgar Square, I journeyed across London the following day to pay back the excess. Rather sadly, the amiable manageress clearly thought I was mad.

But, as I say, my father never questioned his place in the world, either its advantages or its disadvantages. Like Robert, he strove to do his duty and, also like Robert, he thought that if it were God's will that you should be rich, then He would ensure you were left an inheritance. There was something vaguely distasteful to him about striving to make money, as there is to Lord Grantham. He was not, of course, anti-Catholic as Robert is (vaguely), because we are a Catholic family. But I remember him once saying that he thought religions were rather like clubs. There was not much wrong with any of them, but it seemed ill-bred to change. It is something Robert might easily say. And probably will.

I have been accused in the press of being too concerned with class, and thereby a snob. There is some truth to the first, since I am fascinated by the shaping effect of the random selection of class, and how, even today, it has a lasting influence on our aspirations and prospects. A recent report for the Labour Government concluded that birth remained the greatest determinant when it came to our futures in modern Britain. This seems extraordinary to me, partly because I grew up in the 1960s, a generation that assumed all such stuff was coming to an end, and if you had asked anyone in 1968 how important class would be in 40 years' time, they would have laughed in your face. But perhaps I have a greater sensibility because, to a degree, I was brought up in a class minefield. My father's birth was grander than my mother's, his relations therefore disapproving of both her family and her, and she was condemned to the unenviable task of making everything in their life seem smooth and seamless when it was in fact riven with stitching. She was a strong woman and in her youth a great beauty, which is a powerful social tool even if it carries a sell-by date, but it was never plain sailing, all the same. The gap today would not feel wide, she from the respectable middle class, he from what one of my brothers refers to rather caustically as the 'landless gentry', but in 1935, the year of their marriage, it was a chasm. The cool dismissals, the veiled snubs, the cold-shouldering of a friendly gesture, I have witnessed them all, both through the puzzled eyes of childhood, and with the more knowledgeable vision of later on. I suppose standing, as it were, on both sides of the divide has influenced my work, but, as anyone logical could tell, the accusation of snobbery is wide of the mark. It is precisely because I identify with both teams that my writing, if I am allowed to say so, aspires to a kind of social justice which, I believe anyway, is one of the reasons it has reached so wide an audience.

It was the maid of a cousin of my grandfather's, an auxiliary great-aunt to us boys, who inspired O'Brien, one of my favourite characters. She had started out as a lady's maid, but when the old world disintegrated, she graduated to companion and remained in this post until the death of her employer. On the surface, she was as polite as a courtier, but she had a black heart, cold and manipulative, and gradually forced all her mistress's family and friends away, until she ruled their Knightsbridge house alone. Yet my aunt never saw it. As far as she was concerned, she had a faithful retainer who wanted nothing but her good, and she never made the connection with the absence of her family in the later years. I was once told by a viewer that the only detail he didn't recognise from the world of his youth was the devious lady's maid. But the records show he was wrong. As a breed, they were notorious for their complex and prickly nature, fraught with terrors about any possible challenge to their status. Siobhan Finneran gives us a wonderful example of this type; hard, calculating and yet vulnerable when it comes to O'Brien's own feelings. I love her.

And so their parentage continues. Thomas descends from a dresser in my theatrical past. Isobel Crawley owes much to the wife of my godfather, a psychology professor, Carson to my dear friend, Arthur Inch, a retired butler who was the principal advisor on *Gosford Park*, dead now, alas, but a really lovely man. Mrs Hughes I have invented, but she represents what must surely have been the majority of servants who regarded service as just a job; servants who neither hated nor worshipped their employers, and who would meet the different future without either passion or regret. Mary, I have been told, is modelled on my wife, and they are quite similar physically, but I would suggest my indomitable mother plays a part in her, although she and Emma share the quality of shaping their own destiny, rather than abiding by the rules of others.

In fact, they all, I hope anyway, have some corresponding inspiration in the real world, which only goes to make the world of *Downton Abbey* more real. Certainly, it is pretty real to me, and I hope this book will make it even more real to you.

THE EARL & COUNTESS
OF GRANTHAM

THE HOUSEHOLD OF THE EARL OF GRANTHAM

Numbers for the Week ending Sunday, 13ᵗʰ 1920

	BREAKFAST.	LUNCH.	DINNER.	REMARKS.
MONDAY ...	5	5	7	
TUESDAY	4	5	14	
WEDNESDAY ...		5	5	
THURSDAY ...	3	6	5	Preparations
FRIDAY ...	10	14	18	
SATURDAY ...				
SUNDAY	7	7	6	
TOTAL	39			?.

DAILY CARD

22nd 19 20

HOURS	LADY GRANTHAM	LORD GRANTHAM	FAMILY
7 am		Valet	
8 am	Ladies Maid		Lady Mary
Breakfast	Su Room	Dining Room	
9 am			
10 am			
11 am		Chauffeur	
12 pm	Visit Village Hall		
1 pm			
Lunch	Phases		
2 pm			
3 pm		Livery	
4 pm	Arrange displays		
Tea			
5 pm			
6 pm			
7 pm			
8 pm			
Dinner	Js	Js	Lady Mary
9pm		Drawing Room	Lady Edith
10 pm			

Robert It's not so good for you.

Cora Don't worry about me. I'm an American. Have gun, will travel.

Robert Thank God for you, anyway.

Lord Grantham – Robert – has many good qualities: he is kind, loyal to his family, loving to his wife, adoring of his daughters, a fair employer and generous to those around him. But, for him, all these things are peripheral in the face of his most important role in life – as the 7th Earl of Grantham. As he sees it, he has been put on this earth with one prime objective: to keep Downton Abbey in its proper state and hand it over in this condition to his heir. Yet the gods appear to be against him in this enterprise: the American heiress he married to safeguard the future of the estate failed to produce the required son and heir; the next in line (a first cousin) was lost on the *Titanic*, leaving a distant, unknown, middle-class relative – Matthew Crawley – as heir. A brutal war undermined Robert's certainties and prosperity, and now, in the post-war years, he has lost the family fortune in an unwise business venture and faces an uncertain financial future.

Shattered by this recent sequence of events, the mere mention of hiring a new footman is enough to rattle him. Hugh Bonneville, who plays Lord Grantham, explains: 'His purpose is to preserve the estate and hand it on to the next generation. So whenever anything occurs that threatens him and this idea, it sets him off kilter.' For someone as well-meaning as Robert, this situation seems terribly unjust.

It's not all bad. The American heiress he married was, of course, Cora – a woman of resilience and unfailing supportiveness. Where Robert is emotionally insecure, she is sure of herself and undaunted by the difficulties they could face. His daughters may not be able to inherit Downton, but his eldest has done the

next best thing and become engaged – at last – to the man who will. And that man, Matthew, is someone who Robert has grown to love as a son.

If anything gives Robert an advantage in these shifting times, it is probably his marriage to Cora. Elizabeth McGovern, who plays Cora, the Countess of Grantham, says of her character: 'She finds it much easier to assimilate change than Robert, although whether that is because she is an American or because of her character is debatable. But it is this readiness that places her in the middle between her children and the older generation.'

Cora draws Robert into his role as a parent and reminds him that he should mind less about tradition and reputation and more about the happiness of his children. 'Cora is much more able to see Branson as a young man, rather than as a chauffeur,' says McGovern. As a mother, she has a role in life, no matter what else is going on, but being Robert's wife is also very important to her. Cora recognises both her position as countess and the responsibilities that it entails, but also her husband's need for her emotional support. That said, her determination to get stuck into the war effort did mean that she withdrew from her marriage for a time, leaving Robert feeling isolated.

Robert Sometimes I feel like a creature in the wilds, whose natural habitat is gradually being destroyed.

Furthermore, much of what Robert sees around him, and particularly what he reads about in the newspapers, can only serve to underline his fears that he is becoming an outmoded, defunct element of society. As Britain began to recover its senses after the war, it became clear there was no hope of returning to the way things had been in 1914. In 1920 Devonshire House, one of the most famed palaces on Piccadilly (the venue for a party for Queen Victoria's Diamond Jubilee in 1897), was sold by the Duke of Devonshire to a financier. The Duke had been crippled by the debts of his predecessor and the first death duties his family had had to pay, which amounted to around half a million pounds. (The house was later demolished and only the wine cellar and gates remain – the latter form the entrance to Green Park.) The sale of the house marked the end of an era. For Robert it would have been a vivid sign that even the grandest, richest families were not immune to the stringent financial pressures of the post-war world.

Robert You make it sound very serious.
Murray I am expressing myself badly
if you think it is not serious.

One duchess wrote, 'There was a good deal in the Press at the time about the New Poor and the New Rich (the former being admirable and the latter despicable) and the ladies who came to lunch with my mother deplored Modern Times. They said how crippling the taxes were, how dreadful the housing shortage, how expensive the shops, how high the wages, how spoilt the children ... ' There was, in short, an atmosphere of difficulty and change. Many were prone to a sort of depression, a lingering dissatisfaction, referred to as *'le cafard'*. There was a feeling amongst the landed classes that despite having fought and won a war, and sacrificed so many of their sons, they had no place in their country anymore.

Robert How's the wedding going?
I suppose it's costing the earth.
Cora Mary was never going to
marry on the cheap.
Robert Oh, no. Nothing must be
done on the cheap.

Robert's own small kingdom had been turned upside down by Sybil running off with the chauffeur. He is almost unable to reconcile himself to the fact and has to be reminded by Mary to be nicer to Branson, or the village would dine out on the story for evermore. She herself has caused much worry for her parents, but she seems to have found contentment at last in her engagement to the man she loves, although the matter of the cost of her wedding and where she and Matthew will live is weighing heavily upon Robert. Then there's Edith, who seems destined either to be a spinster or to marry a man for whom she must be more nurse than wife. But Robert admires each of his daughters for their individual merits. 'Despite everything, he does have quite liberal tendencies,' says Bonneville. 'He always makes a token gesture of disapproving of his daughters' decisions. Much as he disapproves of Sybil's methods, he admires her spark. And he secretly approves of them ploughing their own furrows – in Edith's case during the war, literally.'

While all these things would unsettle Robert, they are not the main cause for his concern. More pressingly, Robert is facing the fact that he no longer knows quite how to fulfil his role in life, the one thing of which he had always been so certain. During the war, Robert had learnt for the first time how it felt to be useless – and he didn't bear it well. His uniform, worn proudly during the Boer War, had become little more than a costume, each military honour only serving to mock his old age and inadequacy. While his wife and daughters seemed to be busier than ever, genuinely contributing to the war effort, he had nothing to do. And any hope that he could resume his seat of power once the battles were over was soon dashed.

It was this feeling of impotence that led to Lord Grantham's kiss with the maid, Jane, believes Bonneville: 'During the war there was a sense of him losing confidence; of having a dose of the Black Dog. He feels a loss of purpose while Cora and the girls are throwing themselves into war work. His old regiment only want him as a figurehead. And this is what leads to him coming off the rails a bit, morally.' Happily, he gets himself back on track quickly. 'I remember Julian once saying that his default position when writing was that people essentially want to be good,' says Bonneville. 'They can end up doing bad things, but they rarely start with that intention. That is very true of Robert.' He's fortunate, too, in that he and Cora generally have a loving, intimate marriage, unusually sharing a bed every night. As one peeress of the time wrote: 'In a big house, husband and wife could live their own lives without treading on each other's corns. Intimacy was not considered a necessary ingredient of a happy marriage: there is the story of a girl who remarked, on marrying a dull man, that at least she would never have to sit next to him at dinner again.'

At least if Robert bumped into any of his fellow peers at his London club he would have soon realised that his situation was not unique. Almost all members of the aristocracy were feeling the pinch, thanks to massive increases in income tax and death duties (the latter, introduced in 1894 at 8 per cent, had risen to 40 per cent in 1919). Land, the traditional basis of aristocratic wealth, continued to offer poor returns. Agricultural revenues and rents had been declining since the 1880s because of cheap imports from around the world,

while agricultural wages had risen steadily. The process had been exacerbated by the war. Many small estates went to the wall. The old Landed Gentry was decimated. But even large estates struggled. Many aristocrats decided to sell off some of their land in order to raise money to pay off debts or for investments. The years immediately after the First World War saw land sales on an unprecedented scale. Over a million acres changed hands in 1919 and the following year even this record was surpassed, with vast estates sold off by the Dukes of Leeds, Beaufort, Marlborough, Grafton and Northumberland. The Duke of Norfolk sold some 20,000 acres of his Yorkshire estate.

Robert I have a duty beyond saving my own skin. The estate must be a major employer and support the house or there's no point to it. To any of it.

To lose land meant more than losing face or being embarrassed at having failed where ancestors had not. It meant that one was no longer able to serve the local county as a significant employer and landlord, which was the main purpose of a great house. Robert feels the responsibility keenly – his sense of duty towards his tenants and workers is one of the reasons the state of his financial affairs matters so much. It may also be the reason it is in disarray; benign landlords would not be keen to force rents up and thereby push their tenants into hardship. It is Robert's duty as keeper of the estate that shores up his belief in himself and gives meaning to his relationships: he has a deep respect for Carson, with whom he practically shares the responsibility of the house, and in Bates he believes he has crossed the class divide to achieve real friendship. (Although I am not always convinced that Bates shares this feeling in equal measure.)

Besides land and wealth, the British aristocracy had also traditionally enjoyed prestige and political clout. These, too, however, were being fatally undermined. The power of the House of Lords had been greatly reduced by the Parliament Act of 1911, which abolished the right of the Lords to veto bills passed by the House of Commons. The social prestige of the Lords had been compromised by the massive increase in the number of new peers. Lloyd George, the Prime Minister, an implacable foe of the landed aristocracy – together with his fixer,

Maundy Gregory – shamelessly sold off titles to wealthy individuals. The going rate was £10,000 for a knighthood, £30,000 for a baronetcy and £50,000-plus for a peerage. Plutocrats who had made vast fortunes in industry, the City or the Press – and whose wealth now surpassed that of all but the largest landowners – were quick to take advantage. The arrival of such 'new men' was a challenge to the old order. Britain might be becoming more meritocratic and more democratic, but these were unsettling changes for Robert to come to terms with.

Cora A lot of people live in smaller houses than they used to.

Mary Which only goes to show that you are American and I am English.

Cora may not be excited by these changes, but she is quick to react with a positive attitude. As an American, she has a different view of tradition, is less weighed down by the expectations of dead ancestors and is more concerned with ensuring her nearest and dearest are happy than with keeping the ancient roof over their heads. An upbringing surrounded by money has given Cora security and confidence, and having conquered her own realm, on her own terms, she is less frightened by the thought that it could disappear. If she has to do it all again, she will. In fact, she rather relishes the challenge: she, like her daughters Edith and Sybil, found a role for herself during the war and now that it is over, she misses it. When Robert turns to her, she is only too glad to be able to help and regain a more prominent position in her marriage and household. 'She is unbelievably loving and patient with his shortcomings,' says McGovern. 'But then, she is very much in love with him. She fills in the cracks – as we all do with those we love.'

Cora would be glad of the distraction for other reasons. She would have been acutely aware that many of her friends were mourning their sons; one in five aristocrats who went to the war died – a far higher proportion than any other group. (Across the rest of the British forces the ratio was one in eight.) And although the conflict had ended, it was hard not to be haunted by its effects. As the Countess of Fingall recalled, 'I used to think and say during the war that if ever that list of Dead and Wounded could cease, I would never mind anything

or grumble at anything again,' she recalled. 'But when the Armistice came at last, we seemed drained of all feeling. One felt nothing. We took up our lives again or tried to take them up. The world we had known was vanished. We hunted again but ghosts rode with us. We sat at table and there were absent faces.'

There was another, unexpected side-effect of the war. Before, the aristocracy had seemed remote to those of the lower classes, but at the Front they lived side by side in the trenches, while the women worked alongside each other as nurses. Something of the mystique of the aristocracy had been lost. Cora, as an American, is unfazed by this, and perhaps even welcomes the softening of the old rigid hierarchies. But she is also aware of how disturbing such changes must be for Robert.

Like her husband, Cora can draw strength from the fact that she is not alone in her situation. In 1880 (some ten years before her marriage to Robert) there had been only four American peeresses in England; by the time of the First World War there were 50. What is more, the flavour of English social life was becoming increasingly American and informal, thanks to a new generation of transatlantic hostesses – women such as Elsa Maxwell, Nancy Astor and Emerald Cunard. The first 'Buccaneers' marrying into the British aristocracy had found Society intolerably stuffy, with its rigid hierarchies and formal rules. But in the post-war world, things were beginning to loosen up. Cora – in distant Downton Abbey – might be far removed from Lady Cunard's artistic salon in London, but she would have saluted her fellow American's style and achievement.

The prospect of leaving Downton and taking on a smaller house, while sad, gives Cora a satisfying occupation. Before the war, her leisure activities were few. Some women were accomplished painters or needleworkers, but many others passed time making 'spills' – old letters cut into 2–3-inch lengths then folded, concertina-like, into tapers. They would be held in the fire to take light and used instead of a match. 'It was such a pleasant and peaceful occupation to make unwanted letters into spills and fill the boxes,' recalled Lady Hyde Parker. 'The study and library, and also the boudoir, all had spill boxes on their chimney pieces at Melford.'

The war, of course, also changed fashions for women and the general preoccupation with dressing and changing for every small occasion started to lessen. Cora is elegant and sophisticated, maintaining more length to her hemlines than her daughters, so the costume designer looked for dresses that showed her 'American openness to change, mixed with a certain formality'. For one evening dress, they drew up a design inspired by Lanvin, a 1920s designer whose looks harked back to the eighteenth century. 'We used that idea and created a soft pannier effect with netting over a silk under-dress in a dark cherry colour,' explains Caroline McCall. 'I had a beautiful old beaded chiffon panel which had been found by a textile dealer and had the dress made up to incorporate it.'

Robert is more conservative and less responsive to changing fashions, although he would take the lead of his Savile Row tailor. His black tie was made there by Huntsman and doesn't have the narrow waist fashionable in 1920. 'But even so, we've tried to make him move with the times a bit,' says McCall. 'His suits aren't as high-fastening as they were. They have three buttons now, rather than four. He sometimes wears soft collars in his country gear, but usually sports a "double round" and "Albany" or, on formal occasions, a "tipped imperial".'

Violet It's our job to create employment. An aristocrat with no servants is as much use to the county as a glass hammer.

Robert conducts his life at a different pace to those around him, and he is unlikely to speed up in the fast-paced modern world. 'He can afford to have a slower pulse than anyone else,' says Bonneville. 'If you live in a world where the main concern is what you are going to wear for dinner – and you know you will be wearing white tie – you are able to take things more slowly. From the acting point of view, that is one of the key things to hold onto.' The world as Robert knew it in his formative years may be beginning to crumble around him, but he recognises he must try to keep up with the times if he is to live a fulfilling life and support his dependants. With Cora by his side, he has every chance of doing so.

Shooting parties were one of the fixtures – and one of the highlights – of the aristocratic year. They provided a different, less formal atmosphere; what Julian Fellowes characterises as a distinctly British 'elite informality'. As one butler recalled, 'You always had lunch outside ... It was a little more relaxed; you didn't have to be so polite ... the family seemed more relaxed too. It was a different sort of set-up. I enjoyed it.'

Lady Grantham's Cartier diamond necklace is the badge of her class. The great Parisian jewellers, established in 1847, had long owned shops in New York and London; Edward VII had famously declared Cartier to be 'the Jeweller of Kings and the King of Jewellers'. Jewels were an important part of any aristocratic lady's inheritance. At Society weddings the principal presents (which were listed in the newspapers) were the jewels given to the bride, by her parents, her parents-in-law and other distinguished friends. Worn at formal occasions, they proclaimed the couple's wealth and status.

MR CARSON
&
MRS HUGHES

THE BUTLER &
THE HOUSEKEEPER

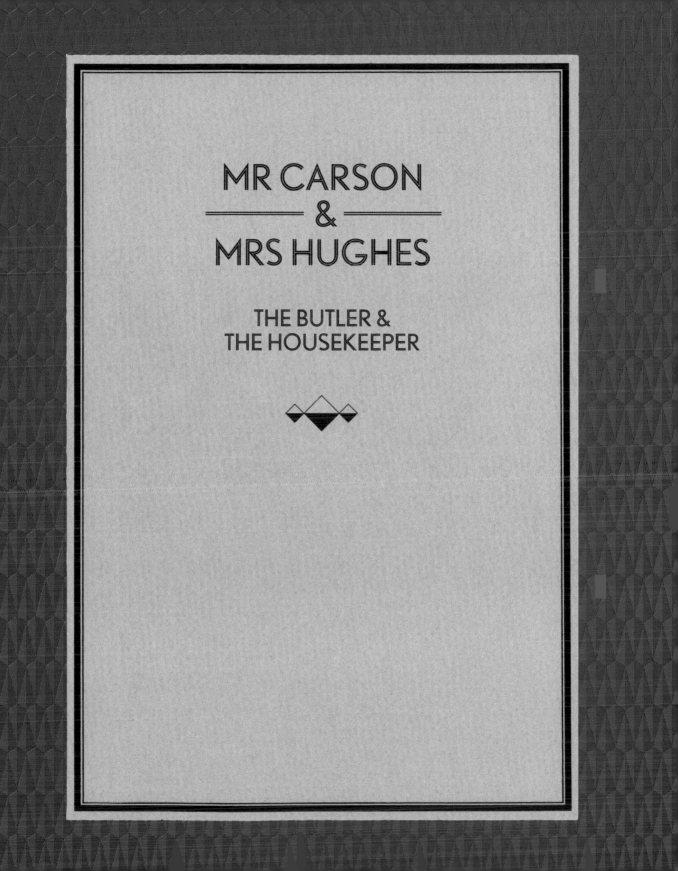

Above: 'The Electric Hotpoint Toaster – what a boon it is!' as the instruction manual declared. In the new world of electric gadgetry the toaster was a relatively late arrival. For its success it required a wire element that would heat quickly to very high temperatures without either catching fire or becoming brittle with repeated use. This was only achieved in 1905 with the development of an alloy of nickel and chromium (at first called 'nichrome' and, subsequently, 'chromel'). The first electric toasters followed soon after. General Electric led the way with their Hotpoint brand. The bread was toasted on one side at a time and had to be flipped either manually or automatically. The first pop-up toaster was patented in 1919, but didn't become commercially available until 1926.

Right: Entertaining was an important element in the life of any great house, and preparations would be undertaken jointly by the butler and the housekeeper. Guests would be assigned their bedrooms by the housekeeper, after discussion with the lady of the house. Guests and their servants would all need to be accommodated; but any visitors staying without staff would be 'looked after' by their host's footmen and housemaids. Valets were allocated by Carson from his male staff, while Mrs Hughes would assign lady's maids from her female staff

Wedding Preparations   VISITORS

Name	Room	Special Requirements	Numbers	Valet or Ladies Maid
The Lady Isabelle	Bristo	No Meat for any meal	1	Ladies Maid
Mr Sallcroft	Arundel		1	
Mrs Arabella	Queen Caroline	breakfast in her room	1	Ladies Maid
Mr Bedingham	Mercia	luggage to follow	2	
The Count of Cresten	East Anglia		1	Valet
The Countess of Cresten	Grantham		2	Ladies Maid
Lord and Lady Delling	Stanhope	Papers to be taken to room every morning	2	Ladies Maid and Valet
Lord and Lady Ansdell	Ripon		2	
Lord Cronqharvet	Wetherby		1	Valet
Sir Fraser Blake	Harrogate		1	Valet
Sir Edward Profue	Bootham			

Carson What in God's name is it?
Mrs Hughes An electric toaster.
I've given it to myself as a treat.
If it's any good, I'm going to suggest
we get one for the upstairs breakfasts.

The delivery of a toaster to Downton Abbey heralds the arrival of post-war technology and the beginning of changes below stairs, and unsurprisingly Carson is reluctant to receive it. A man with a strong faith in tradition, he cannot see the good that can come of anything new. Mrs Hughes, however, being the rather more pragmatic one of the pair, fully embraces innovation if it means she can do her job more efficiently.

The butler is very clear about his role in life: it is to keep the house running along the same lines that it always has. 'Carson comes from a family of soldiers and servants,' says Julian Fellowes. 'His grandfather was a head groom and so he's middle-middle class – they certainly weren't scrabbling in the gutter for food.' Carson is a firm believer in monarchy, the aristocracy and social order – everyone has a place, as he sees it, and he is keen that they keep to it.

As we discovered in Series 1, Carson left behind an embarrassing past as half of the music hall act 'Cheerful Charlies' to enter service. Jim Carter, who plays Carson, explains the effect this dramatic career change has had on the character: 'People who escape from one thing into something else can be the most zealous disciples. Carson is like that. He has buried his past life and loves Downton – a world where there is a place for everything and everything is in its place.'

With the war over and victory secured, Carson hopes that things might return to how they were – in this he, Lord Grantham and the Dowager Countess are united. (Carson's clothes do not even change one jot during the entire three series – 'unchanged and unchanging, just as he would like it', says the costume designer, Caroline McCall.) But he is beginning to realise that he

may be disappointed. Quite apart from the fact that the house is understaffed, meaning that no event can be carried out in the style to which he is accustomed (he minds this particularly for Lady Mary and Matthew Crawley's wedding), the war has changed things in another, more fundamental way. Those who fought in the trenches have returned with a new attitude to life. Matthew's pronouncements that he wants to 'live in a simpler way' do not bode well for the likes of Carson and his approach to doing things.

Mrs Hughes The world does not turn on the style of a dinner.
Carson My world does.

Carson is ruffled when things veer off course, whether it's maids in the dining room, the thought of an absence of footmen for a Society wedding or the chauffeur sleeping above stairs as the husband of the Earl's youngest daughter. While he may bear some of life's harsher challenges with cool composure and British reserve – including war, death and leaving Downton Abbey – the sight of an inexperienced footman trying to serve the Dowager Countess potatoes sends him into a tailspin.

Carson needs more footmen, but they are 'thinner on the ground than before the war', as O'Brien reminds him, and their role is an exacting one, which means suitable candidates are not easily found. The usual channels – an agency in London, an advertisement in *The Times*, the 'underground network' (through which he could ask butlers in other households if they knew of anyone suitable) – fail to yield any results in 1920. When O'Brien suggests her nephew, Alfred Nugent, he is not averse to the idea, but he is taken off-guard when O'Brien fixes it so that Lady Grantham sanctions the appointment behind his back. Carson could not find the Countess at fault – he may concede that as an American she may not realise that this is the wrong way to go about things, but he knows that O'Brien has deliberately foxed him.

A butler expected to have absolute control in his domain, which included the hiring and firing of the male servants (Mrs Hughes was in charge of the female servants), and he would inform the mistress of the house of his decisions. (Of course, neither have much say over the other upper servants: the valet, lady's maid and cook.) Patricia, Viscountess Hambleden, explained how the butler at

Wilton House during her youth would manage things: 'If he felt somebody was really unsatisfactory, he would come and say, "I'm afraid George is no good. I think you'd better get rid of him," and he would then find somebody else.'

Mrs Hughes gave up the idea of marriage and a family for her career as Downton's housekeeper. We don't know why, but we can suppose she planned a life for herself more compelling than that of her predecessors, working as tenant farmers. She certainly doesn't seem to have thrown in her lot with the Suffragettes: we never see her cornering Sybil for a discussion, let alone being sympathetic to any housemaid who expresses a desire to leave service.

This does not mean she was without ambition: a career in service was something to be proud of; the job was steady, she had respect from her colleagues and she could look forward to a reasonably comfortable retirement provided by the Downton Abbey estate, if she served the family for many years. She even has enough money and interest to spend on her look. For the third series the costume department have given her a dress that is 'slightly more fashionable. The necklines are just a bit lower, and the hemlines higher,' says McCall. It's not what you'd call racy, but nor is it completely dowdy.

There was just one thing that could undermine a housekeeper's carefully laid plans and that would be if she were to fall ill. Quite apart from the worry of being sick, if she were unable to work her accommodation would come under question. There would be no house of her own, and for the likes of Mrs Hughes at least, no apparent family ready to take her in. At that time there was only very limited state provision – it could not hope to keep anyone comfortable for long.

While Mrs Hughes has no enemies below stairs, she doesn't have any close friends either. 'There is a touch of Calvinist certainty about her,' says Phyllis Logan, the actress portraying the housekeeper. 'She has to maintain a certain stance with her girls. She doesn't want them to see her as lax, or a soft touch.' In times of personal trouble, there are few to whom Mrs Hughes can turn. As housekeeper, it wasn't done to confide in any of the junior servants. Carson is her professional peer, but as a male colleague there is a line between them that cannot be crossed. In the end, despite their tussles in the past, whether over the kitchen store cupboard keys or the cost of groceries, Mrs Hughes turns to Mrs Patmore. They have worked in the same household for several years and they know each other well. Professionally, they occupy separate domains, so they can keep their distance when they need to, but right now Mrs Hughes needs a sympathetic ear. It's just a pity that the brusque Mrs Patmore might not have the kind of bedside manner one would hope for at a time like this.

In many ways, Carson and Mrs Hughes are the mirror image of Lord and Lady Grantham. The Earl may be the master of the estate but it is Carson who is master of the house. The Countess may oversee the social life of the family and invite guests, but it is Mrs Hughes who ensures that visitors enjoy a comfortable and impressive stay. But however much Carson and Mrs Hughes respect the Granthams and enjoy their own superior positions, and however much the Granthams are grateful to their butler and housekeeper for doing their jobs well, neither party crosses the line and encourages any intimate familiarity.

Mrs Hughes As you know, I don't worship them all like you do —

Carson Well, I wouldn't put it like —

It is a strange life for the likes of Carson and Mrs Hughes, sitting between the family and the servants and never completely belonging to either group. It's easy to understand why the two of them seek refuge in each other, even in their own rather stilted fashion. But although they are relatively close (are there not shades of *The Remains of the Day* in their relationship, now and then?), they do find fault with one another. Mrs Hughes thinks Carson snobbish in his attitudes at times, while Carson thinks Mrs Hughes is unreasonably impatient with the family, asking them to do things that are not in their gift. To make his point, he could recommend to her a popular film that came out just the year before, in 1919. *Male and Female* (based on J. M. Barrie's 1902 play *The Admirable Crichton*) features a Lord Loam and his family and staff, shipwrecked on a desert island. The butler, Crichton, is the most practical and adaptable member of the group – Carson would have enjoyed that – and becomes its leader. Lady Mary, Lord Loam's daughter, falls in love with him. (Carson would have felt a bit unsure at this point. Mrs Hughes would raise an eyebrow.) They are about to get married when a passing boat spots them, and they are all rescued. The wedding is called off as they revert to their accustomed places in the social hierarchy on their return to civilisation. And Carson would consider that a very happy ending indeed.

Despite his avuncular position below stairs, Carson can be unmerciful when it comes to human fallibilities, unless the person concerned is either an aristocrat who plays by the rules or a professionally brilliant servant, in which case he forgives them everything. 'He's not a tartar,' says Carter of Carson. 'But getting

Carson I am not dressing a chauffeur.

Mrs Hughes He is not a chauffeur now.
Anyway, you don't have to dress him.
Just see he's got everything he needs.

things right is important to him. People must be good at their jobs.' He knows, for example, that Thomas stole wine from the stores and is an arrogant, sly character, but because he cannot find anyone who can be as good a valet as he can (in Bates's absence), he encourages Lord Grantham to take him on. Although Carson initially took against Bates on the grounds that his limp and walking stick would mean he couldn't do his job properly, now that he has worked with him, and knows better, the fact that the valet is locked up in prison for murder is not enough for Carson to waver even a smidgen in his protection of him.

Carson May I remind you, Mr Barrow, that in this house Mr Bates is a wronged man seeking justice. If you have any problems with that definition, I suggest you eat in the yard.

Carson's seniority is reflected in the tasks that are entrusted to him – cleaning the fine pieces of silver, managing the cellar (choosing and ordering the wines and port, then deciding which would be served at each lunch and supper), and decanting and pouring the wine. Often, filming the role is as tedious as some of a butler's working hours must have been. Carter explains: 'For me, the upstairs work is harder, because I have less to do. I'm literally standing around for most of the day, before passing someone a dish or pouring out some wine. It is very tiring and the time drags. But it is also very much what it must have been like being a butler. Downstairs, he's the centre of attention. He walks into a room and everyone jumps to attention. The days filming those scenes at Ealing fly by!'

Over and above any duties, the butler felt a sense of responsibility for the running of the entire household. The work of the footmen had to be overseen, the needs of the family had to be ascertained and attended to, the family silver and her ladyship's jewels had to be kept secure, locked in a safe in his pantry, and standards in general had to be maintained. This meant a butler was never off duty. The Duke of Richmond remembered the old butler at his seat, Goodwood: 'I said to him once, "I'm worried about you. I want to see how far you walk." So I got one of those pedometers and put it in his pocket, and found he'd walked 19½ miles in one day, all over the house.'

Striking the right balance between authority over the servants and enforcing a dictatorship, which would only encourage rebellion, was a challenge for a butler, although it is one which Carson has managed. In other houses the battle lines were more starkly drawn. One footman remembered the lengths to which he went to subvert the authority of his butler, Mr Petit: 'He was a cunning bugger; his office was near the front door and, knowing we could hear him as he came from there to the pantry, he'd sometimes take his boots off and walk in his stockinged feet expecting, even I think hoping, to find that we were up to no good. I was able to sort him out for a time. There was a loose tile under the rug outside his room; I ran a wire there and connected it up to a bell in the pantry so that when he left we were given a timely warning. I can still feel the pain on my backside when I recall the day he discovered it.'

The satisfaction of seeing a job well done is one that Carson takes pleasure in. One butler recounted the pride he took in overseeing the setting of a table for a dinner party. 'Assuming the guests have been brought up to it and know what to expect, they will sit at that table in complete comfort. Everything they need is to hand. There's no stretching for anything, no knocking things over when they're reaching for something else. It's a matter of where you put glasses and plates, and the decorative effect as well. There's ways you do things so that you don't forget anything. Scrabbling around moving stuff while people are actually sitting there is not really on!'

Most of all, Carson delights in being surrounded by fine things. He would endorse the sentiments of the butler who saw his working life as an education: 'It was impossible to live amongst beauty without it getting under your skin; you learn to distinguish what is good and what is not; you learn taste and appreciation; you look at books lining shelves and eventually you pick one up and begin to read; overheard conversations spark off a desire to know more. You also learn moral values, not always by example but by observation and comparison.'

Mrs Hughes appears to have less truck with this view. We don't hear her express an interest in European royal families, much less admire the pictures hanging in the great hall. She is more likely scanning them for any dust collecting in the curlicues of the gilt frames. Of all the servants, Mrs Hughes appears to do the least. She is often spotted walking briskly through a room, pausing to question a junior housemaid on her work, keys jangling at her side, but it's not absolutely apparent what she is there to do. In fact, there are myriad things for her to think about, beginning with supervising the housemaids in their daily round of fire-laying, sweeping and dusting, ensuring all the public rooms are

ready before breakfast. After that, the beds must be made (sheets were changed once a week; the mistress's changed twice), and the water carafes refreshed. There would be rotas to draw up and monitor, from the female servants' duties to the linens, and ensuring the principal rooms are cleaned thoroughly in turn.

The linens would take up a great deal of the housekeeper's time. Aside from bed linen there was an arsenal of 'working linen' to be ordered, prepared and maintained. The kitchen needed tea towels for drying dishes, oven cloths, round towels for drying hands, fine-linen cloths for straining soups and a host of other scraps. The housemaids required their own set of cloths and towels; the butler and footmen used an endless supply of linen towels as well as thin, pure-linen squares for drying the silver. All these would be used regularly, and house-keepers would often be up until midnight preparing them for the week ahead.

Mrs Hughes is also in charge of the house stores. Soap powders and so on could be ordered quarterly in bulk from London, but other items would come from local suppliers. Mrs Hughes's eye might be drawn to ads in the paper tempt-ing her to try something new, such as Stephenson's Furniture Cream – 'Gives a mirror-like polish which will not fingermark'. She's not fazed by progress and seems eager to try out new labour-saving devices. When she travelled to London to help Anna prepare Bates's house for letting at the start of 1920, she could have visited the Ideal Home Exhibition. The theme reflected the 1919 Housing Act, which promised 'homes fit for heroes', so the emphasis was on domestic hygiene and labour-saving features. Mrs Hughes might have fancied the 'all-electric tea table' for her sitting room, featuring a toast rack, electric kettle and heating stand.

A major perk of being the housekeeper was the 'tip' or 'commission' she received back from the suppliers that she favoured with her custom. Mrs Bristow, the housekeeper at Thorpe-Sackville in Leicestershire between the wars, recalled how the system worked: she would take all bills – signed by herself – to the master or mistress, who would then write out cheques for the various tradesmen. 'If you paid within the week sometimes I've had as much as 30 shillings back from the fishmonger and greengrocer.'

Mrs Hughes arrived at Downton Abbey after the present Lord and Lady Grantham had installed themselves, and it is their vision for the house that she seeks to fulfil. This arrangement worked well, as established housekeepers tended to get set in their ways and could sometimes resent the arrival of a new mistress. The Viscountess of Hambleden wrote that when she first arrived at Greenlands (her husband's home), the incumbent housekeeper tried to under-mine and humiliate her in small ways. One of her ploys was to give the grandest

At the annual festive Servants' Ball, employers and staff cast aside social barriers for one night and enjoy Downton Abbey together.

guests inferior cotton sheets rather than the best linen ones. Fortunately, she soon left.

As with Carson, Mrs Hughes's biggest challenge after the war is retaining servants and finding new ones. A whole generation of young women had experienced a life of camaraderie and relative freedom in various war-time employments – munitions factories and other industries, agriculture and office work – and they weren't anxious to give up this newfound liberty. There was also an increasing feeling that service might be a demeaning career. One reluctant recruit, on taking up her position as third housemaid in a large house at Argyllshire, said her 'greatest horror' was 'the knowledge that I would now have to submit to the badge of servitude – a cap and apron'. There was even an article in *The Lady* (a weekly magazine used then, as now, for placing ads for vacant domestic situations) in 1919 with the title 'Why I Dislike Domestic Service'. The various objections were listed: '1. It means loss of caste; 2. It means loss of freedom of action – a girl was not on her own; 3. Long hours when they are on duty, if not actually working; 4. It was dull, the work was fairly hard, and distinctly monotonous.'

Mrs Hughes We can't do things properly until either his lordship allows us the staff we need, or until you and the blessed Lady Mary come down from that cloud and join the human race!

For the time being, Carson and Mrs Hughes are content to stay at Downton as joint rulers of their own below-stairs kingdom, enjoying respect and relative comfort. Mrs Hughes faces uncertainty about her future because of her ill health, but she can depend on those around her to keep her safe. For Carson, the threat to his security lies in his need for the old-world order to return. As the heads of the European monarchies topple he foresees a knock-on effect that could lead to his loss of livelihood and home, and the displacement of those he knows and loves. To keep his world turning, Carson fixes his attention on the things he can make a difference to: making sure the right wine is decanted, the footmen are in their livery and the silver is polished to a high gleam.

Mrs Hughes is never separated from her keys.
She was guardian of the store-cupboards, controlling
the supplies of food, cleaning products and linen for the
household. They were all valuable commodities which
were kept under lock and key.

Carson has a proper reverence for the royal family and
the sense of continuity that they provide in a changing
world. 'It was stabilising for the nation', explains Julian Fellowes,
'to have a pre-war king on the throne after the war was over.'

LADY
MARY CRAWLEY

TRUMPET VOLUNTARY (Op.6 No.5) by John Stanley

FIRST HYMN:

O perfect Love, all human thought transcending,
Lowly we kneel in prayer before Thy throne,
That theirs may be the love which knows no ending,
Whom Thou forevermore dost join in one.

O perfect Life, be Thou their full assurance,
Of tender charity and steadfast faith,
Of patient hope and quiet, brave endurance,
With childlike trust that fears nor pain nor death.

Grant them the joy which brightens earthly sorrow;
Grant them the peace which calms all earthly strife,
And to life's day the glorious unknown morrow
That dawns upon eternal love and life

THE MARRIAGE SERVICE
(The Congregation standing)

The hymns chosen by Lady Mary were both staples of Society weddings – and still are. Indeed, 'Love Divine All Loves Excelling'– with words by Charles Wesley and music by W. P. Rowlands – was sung at the marriage of Prince William and Catherine Middleton.

SECOND HYMN

Love Divine, all loves excelling,
Joy of heaven, to earth come down,
Fix in us thy humble dwelling,
All thy faithful mercies crown.
Jesus, thou art all compassion,
Pure unbounded love thou art;
Visit us with thy salvation,
Enter every trembling heart.

Come, almighty to deliver,
Let us all thy grace receive;
Suddenly return, and never,
Never more thy temples leave.
Thee we would be always blessing,
Serve thee as thy hosts above,
Pray, and praise thee, without ceasing,
Glory in thy perfect love.

Finish then thy new creation
Pure and spotless let us be;
Let us see thy great salvation,
Perfectly restored in thee,
Changed from glory into glory,
Till in heaven we take our place,
Till we cast our crowns before thee,
Lost in wonder, love, and praise!

PRAYERS
During the signing of the register the organist will play from:
Beethoven's "PASTORAL" SYMPHONY

Martha The world has changed.
These houses were built for another age.
Are you quite sure you want to continue
with the bother of it all?
Mary Quite sure.

O f all the characters, Mary is the one who undergoes the greatest meta-
morphosis over the course of the three series. When we first met her
she appeared to be a hard-hearted, rather cold and ambitious elder
daughter of an earl. Blighted by having been born a girl rather than a boy, she
needed to prove that she could make a success of herself just as much as any male
heir would have. But Mary is also traditional in her outlook – closer to her grandmother, the Dowager Countess, than to her American mother – and so seeks
to establish her own power and wealth through a suitable marriage. However,
finding herself engulfed in a potentially ruinous scandal when her one-night
lover, Kemal Pamuk, died in her bed, she was forced to see that even upright
and good people make mistakes. Owing the protection of her reputation to the
discretion and generosity of her servant, Anna, allowed Mary to see altruism in
its purest form. Having to confess her sin to those she most loved and respected –
her father, her grandmother, Matthew – and then living with the knowledge that
several people knew what had happened, exposed her to the pity and forgiveness
of others. These were things which she had neither wanted nor needed before.
Yet, ultimately, the scandal was Mary's salvation, softening her and opening her
up to true, honest love.

Mary was taken by surprise when she fell for Matthew. She knew it would be
convenient for everyone if she did marry him, but she did not think at first that she
could love a man who had not been born into the aristocracy. A man who worked
for his living was not her type, but his kindness of heart, his palpable love for her
and, perhaps, his good looks and charm too, won her over.

Still, it was hard for Mary to relinquish her dream of securing a powerful and rich Society figure for a husband. When it looked as if there was a chance Matthew might not be the heir after all – when Cora was briefly pregnant – Mary wobbled a little. We shouldn't judge her too harshly for this; it takes more to make a happy marriage than love. A shared background and a shared direction for the future matter a great deal, too. Mary had also been schooled in the success of a financially astute match: it was what had happened to her own parents. In the rest of her life Mary is unsentimental – she is less concerned with her popularity than she is with getting what she and her family need. She was quickly punished for these doubts; Matthew sensed her wavering and called off the engagement, and by the next time she saw him, he was in love with Lavinia Swire.

Having her heart both broken and put back together by her true love, Matthew, has rounded the edges off Mary yet more. 'The thought of losing Matthew had a big effect on her,' says Michelle Dockery, the actress playing Mary. 'It made her a nicer person in the end.' Now, she has her backbone of steel but she is kinder, nicer and altogether more forgiving of human fallibilities – even her own. And, of course, she has her own wedding to look forward to, with all the attendant dresses and details to think about and plan. What could be better? But with Mary's headstrong, stubborn temperament and Matthew's desire to toe the moral line, we should not expect their marriage to be free from drama.

The depths to which Mary sank – after the death of Kemal Pamuk – and from which she has now been rescued, should not be belittled as we observe the situation from our twenty-first-century viewpoint. A hundred years ago the idea that an unmarried woman could take a lover was considered immoral, if not perverse, an insult to her femininity and the maternal role for which she was born. Marie Stopes wrote the controversial *Married Love* in 1918, a book intended to aid family planning but which also encouraged a healthy sex life in marriage. In it she says: 'The idea that woman is lowered or "soiled" by sexual intercourse is still deeply rooted in some strata of our society ... Women's education and the trend of social feeling have largely been in the direction of encouraging the idea that sex-life is a low, physical and degrading necessity which a pure woman is above enjoying.'

So when Edith discovered Mary's sordid secret she was delighted – it was the sort of thing that could undermine her elder sister's position in Society in a way that little else could. Their relationship now is less antagonistic than it was, but they will never be close; they are too much set in their pattern. 'Mary is very headstrong and unable to accept that she can't have her own way,' says Julian

Fellowes. 'But coupled to that is that she cannot be pitied. She can never be in a position where anyone feels sorry for her.'

Of her youngest sister, Mary is protective. She may not agree with her politics, but she sees that they both essentially want the same thing – to be happy – they are just going about it in different ways. She worries, too, that Sybil may have made choices that she is unable to make a success of. 'When she discovered Sybil running away with Branson, Mary was playing the part of the older sister,' says Dockery. 'There was also perhaps an element of her stopping someone else from finding happiness by following their heart rather than their head. Which, of course, is what she should have done with Matthew from the beginning.'

Mary is old-fashioned in many respects, closest to her traditional-thinking father ('In some ways she is the son he never had,' says Dockery) and grandmother, and understands their world view in a way that many of her contemporaries do not. This leads her to be sometimes rather dismissive of her mother; Mary does not consider herself half-American but wholly English, and she has no compunction in telling Cora this, more than once. Dockery says of their relationship: 'She acts a little superior around her mother. She shows a sort of teenager's toughness that has never worn off.' If she appreciates her mother for anything, it's the money that she brought to the family, saving the estate.

Mary But I do hope you feel that Mama's fortune has been well spent in shoring up an ancient family.

Martha You gotta spend it on something.

Mary's closest relationships are with men: her father, Matthew and Carson. This stems, perhaps, from her feeling that she should have been born a boy. If she wasn't one, then she was going to be as near as dammit. Her admirable qualities are ones that would have been considered masculine in 1920: she's an adventurer, brave, an excellent horsewoman and a natural leader. In many ways, a woman of her disposition at that time would have been frustrated by the stemming of her potential. It's Mary's archaic views, her determination

to gain power through her role as a châtelaine, that enable her to believe that she can be a success. It's a big contrast to Matthew, whose modern attitude is likely to be what saves Downton Abbey and keeps it a relevant enterprise in the 1920s.

Carson It's not her fault if something has gone wrong.

Mrs Hughes We all know who you think is in the wrong when Lady Mary is involved. The other person.

As a child, Mary would have gone below stairs frequently to enjoy the less formal atmosphere of the servants' hall and kitchens. Carson has been the butler at Downton all her life and she is very fond of him, as he is of her. 'He is another father figure to her,' says Dockery. 'When it comes to emotional matters, she goes to Carson rather than to anyone else. She can be honest and vulnerable in front of him.' This was not unusual even then; upper-class children were often almost entirely brought up by the servants and their nanny, seeing their parents for just a brief moment when they came downstairs from the nursery to be presented at six o'clock in the evening. Cora was probably rather more hands-on as a mother than most of her British peers, but there still would have been plenty of time for Mary to form friendships among the household. Anna is the only other person in front of whom Mary will let down her guard. 'Behind closed doors they can be honest with each other. They can shed a tear together, or share good news,' says Dockery. 'They know each other so well, they can sense if anything is amiss. In the modern world, they would be friends, going to have coffee together and talking about their husbands.'

But while Mary's relationships occupy a great deal of her time, her appearance is also a subject that draws her attention. Her interest in clothes is more than just about following fashion, although that too has its place. One peeress wrote at the time: 'There was nothing for the women to do all day except change their clothes, which they did as if they were odalisques trying to fascinate a pasha, instead of respectable matrons tied to British gentlemen whose minds were

For all her femininity, Mary has strengths that many at the time would have considered masculine, and a fearlessness that helps her to achieve the power she so desires.

entirely fixed on guns, dogs and birds.' After the war, dressing did get simpler – outfits were not changed so frequently, and clothes and underwear became less fussy and easier to get in and out of. But there was still much to think about, for the costume department and also for Liz Trubridge, producer: 'In this series things are changing, which is reflected in the new costumes and hairstyles – and new inventions. Probably the most striking change is the way the upstairs ladies look – the Marcel waves, the looser costumes.'

Hems were rising, going from an inch or two above the floor to above the knee in just a few years (they are calf-length in 1920) – 'There were endless jokes about the shortness of skirts,' said the Duchess of Westminster. There was a move towards a more boyish look, too, with dresses cut to abolish the waistline and bosoms bound as flat as possible by bandeau corsets. Coco Chanel was just beginning her brilliant career, with her 'chemise dress' causing a sensation at the end of 1919. *Vogue* described it as 'a gown that swathes the figure in straight soft folds, falling at the sides in little cascades'; it was considered remarkable for its daring simplicity and its redefinition of femininity, a world away from the pre-war taste for exaggerated and artificial curves.

Robert What's this for?

Mary Going-away. How does it look?

Robert Expensive.

Mary Twice the National Debt, I'm afraid, but I know you don't mind.

Doubtless drawing inspiration from the new weekly fashion magazine *Eve*, Mary shows her sense of style by patronising Madame Vionnet, a Parisian house set at 222 rue de Rivoli, which reopened after the war. It was a Mecca for lovers of beautiful dresses and was the only serious contemporary rival to Chanel. With their halter-necks, flowing lines, wrapped waists, decorated necklines and precise detailing, Vionnet's dresses struck a note of timeless yet utterly modern elegance. If she did not invent the bias cut, she certainly revolutionised its use and its possibilities, creating gowns that hugged the figure and followed its

curves, even in movement. Her clothes gave the wearers a delicious new sense of freedom and a chic touch. A beautiful red, sleeveless evening dress seen on Mary in Series 3 is a copy of a Vionnet piece.

This background gave Caroline McCall an exciting starting point to create Mary's wardrobe. 'I've tried to make her more mature and stylish in her wardrobe,' says McCall. 'She's grown up now, she's getting married and she's going to be a countess.' With her alabaster complexion, Dockery suits strong colours – blues and burgundies – which also work well for her character, 'but we also tried to soften her look a bit, as she is softening'. Each of the daughters has been given their own palette (Edith's is ambers, ochres, greens and pale pinks; Sybil's is mauves and blues), so that they are not only distinct but complementary when together. They also follow distinct fashions: Mary favours designers who dress Society women, Sybil's look is more bohemian and political, while Edith's reflects her practical nature. In so many ways, they are what they wear.

Dulcie Scott, costume supervisor, explains that they looked beyond the fashion books for ideas: 'For all the girls we looked a lot at paintings from the period. Philip de Lázsló portraits have been a big influence.' 'Fashion was becoming more of a thing; there were more magazines, it had a wider appeal and a wider following,' says McCall. 'And as styles became simpler, the quality – of materials, of detail, of making – became more important.'

As much as possible, the costume department tries to use stock pieces, whether in their original state or altered. 'But this is a period where there isn't a great deal around,' explains McCall. 'Either it hasn't lasted – chiffon with beading tends to fall to pieces under its own weight over time – or the dresses were re-structured at a later date because the materials were so fine and expensive. Also, there is the problem that the clothes have to look new to the people who are wearing them. They've got to look fabulous.'

The dress that everyone will be waiting with bated breath to see is the wedding dress. McCall explains the complex issues behind it: 'From our research, I knew that satin and lace were the key things in wedding dresses at the time. We settled on an evening dress shape that I liked, a tabard, one that could be dressed up with a train. I always had this idea of a metallic lace effect – I wanted her to shimmer, unlike anything we had seen before.' Swarovski supplied the stones and they were all hand-stitched onto the dress. The wedding tiara came from Bentley & Skinner, the jewellers on Piccadilly, lending the production a piece that came from 1830. Arriving on its original frame, it would have been worn high up on top of the head, but McCall was able to alter the frame so that it could

be worn lower down on the head, as was the fashion in 1920. Valued at £125,000, a designated person had to be hired to look after it at all times on set.

Hairstyles, too, reflected this novel sensation of liberty in dress. Hair had been getting shorter, a trend that partly began when women working in factories and farms had had to cut their long hair for practicality. But again, Chanel led the way. She cut off her own hair because, she said, 'it annoyed me'. Her stylish 'bob' became a fashion template, but other popular styles were the 'shingle' (when the hair is gradually cut shorter to a 'v' in the nape of the neck) and the 'Eton crop' (a very slicked-down short haircut, much like a schoolboy's).

Make-up began to make more of an appearance in this bold new decade, although as one grande dame recalled, 'It was considered frightfully *mal vu*.' When the American Lady Bingham appeared at a lunch wearing a hat full of artificial cherries and lipstick to match, there was much tutting of disapproval; 'Why didn't she have a discreet colour, instead of cherry red?' Nevertheless, skilfully applied pale powder and lipstick was acceptable on women other than actresses or prostitutes, which was quite a development in itself.

Permanent waving was 'a fairly new process and was as painful as going to the dentist'. The pain that must be endured to create temporary hairstyles was almost as bad – the Marcel-wave curling tongs would become almost unbearably hot, often burning the hair, but the temperature could not be successfully regulated because if they were used when too cool the curls would not 'set'.

Mary travels down to London rather more than her sisters and stays with her aunt, Lady Rosamund Painswick, if not in her father's house in St James's Square. These trips are in part what makes her more comfortable in the world of fashion, and certainly London is where she likes to shop. But there were other entertainments there, too. The Summer Exhibition at the Royal Academy in 1920 had four portraits of fashionable young women as a highlight, reported the *Illustrated London News*. Mary might have gone to see if any of her friends were featured. Going to art exhibitions was seen as a suitable activity for debutantes, particularly when they could see charming fantasies such as the one by the fashionable portraitist Charles Sims: *The Fairies Ran Away With Their Clothes*. But the picture of the year was Sargent's 'haunting and horrible *Gassed*, files of blinded soldiers groping their way across a battlefield'. The war and all its horror was never far away in the minds of those living then, having a sobering effect on any thoughts of gaiety.

The surviving heroes were fêted. T. E. Lawrence (known as Lawrence of Arabia) was celebrated in 1919 for his derring-do in the war. That year, Mary could have gone to London's Royal Opera House for the opening night of a film about him, *With Allenby in Palestine and the Liberation of Holy Arabia*, attended by the Prime Minister Lloyd George, most of the Cabinet and a hand-picked audience of Very Distinguished People. In an unprecedented move, newspaper editors cleared the front pages of ads (stories did not appear on the front at that time) and instead ran the review for the show when it transferred for a run at the Albert Hall. Crowds in their hundreds, desperate for a ticket, brought portable stools and sat all day outside the box office in the hope of a seat. King George V even requested a performance at Balmoral, where he and Queen Mary were spending the summer. Back home, of course, the heroes were being looked after, none more so than Matthew. Mary had been deeply shaken by the fear she felt when he was on the frontline, and although she was not as directly involved in the war effort as her sisters, she was never far from the horror.

Cora Accepting change is quite as important as defending the past.

Mary But the role of houses like Downton is to protect tradition. That's why they're so important to maintain.

'She began as quite an arrogant young girl. She was shaken and vulnerable after the incident with Kemal Pamuk. That vulnerability opened her up, and put her in touch with her emotions rather more,' says Dockery. 'But that practical side she has is still there, and it comes back in this series.' As one part of her life finds resolution, another seems to be unravelling, but Mary is a force to be reckoned with and we know that she will fight for her family's future, whatever the cost.

For a young woman interested in fashion, like Lady Mary, *Vogue* became indispensable reading during the 1920s. Established in America at the end of the nineteenth century, a British edition was launched in 1916 and a French one in 1920. They all provided detailed coverage of French couture at a time when the industry was being transformed through the creations of inspired designers such as Madame Vionnet and Coco Chanel.

The family tiara would have been worn by numerous Crawley brides in the years since its creation in 1830. A beautiful garland of leaves and floral clusters, pavé set with old-cut diamonds, it could also be converted into two brooches, to allow it to be used more often.

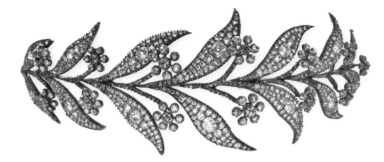

MR THOMAS BARROW

VALET TO THE
EARL OF GRANTHAM

The invention of cigarette-making machinery at the end of the nineteenth century ushered in an age of cheap cigarettes. Cigarette smoking, rather than pipe smoking, became the great working-class pastime and a feature of breaks from work for people like Thomas. Immediately after the war there was a massive surge in consumption and by 1920 over 36 million cigarettes were being smoked in the UK, making huge fortunes for producers such as the Wills family.

Thomas All my life they've pushed me around, just 'cause I'm different.

Thomas Barrow is one of the most complicated and intriguing of all the characters at Downton Abbey. As we have got to know him through years of both peace and war, multiple layers have been peeled away to reveal an insecure, jealous, sometimes paranoid, defensive and cowardly man beneath a glossy veneer of good looks and arrogance. Nor is this the end to his complexity, for in rare, unguarded moments he has revealed he has a heart that is capable of being broken. One wouldn't know it otherwise.

Having survived the First World War, Thomas is, perhaps surprisingly, still to be found at Downton Abbey. Despite his constant bristling against life in service, he never seems able to leave the fold entirely. Life on the outside doesn't appear to suit him. He failed in his one brief try at business and now, having convinced Lord Grantham that he has changed into an honest man, he's been promoted to valet in Bates's absence.

No longer tethered to the butler's pantry nor working under the control and watchful eye of Carson, Thomas has joined the select group of upper servants, which includes the cook, the lady's maid, the butler and the housekeeper. Nor is he in his handsome livery anymore. He remains, however, as vain as ever; his suit is more contemporary than Bates's was as valet. 'He has single-pleat trousers and a three-button jacket, rather than the four buttons his predecessor would have worn,' says Caroline McCall. 'The jacket has a nipped-in waist and so do the trousers. His collars are more modern: an Albany rather than Bates's double round. And he has a special fine-leather glove to cover his wounded hand.'

He might look slightly less striking out of his footman's livery and dressed instead in an ordinary suit, but he is proudly conscious of his promotion, a role that both he and Molesley have long aspired to. Moreover, his new job as a 'body servant' gives him far greater knowledge of his master's affairs – knowledge that might prove useful to him, and of interest to his old ally, O'Brien.

But in post-war Downton we discover that O'Brien's loyalties have shifted from Thomas to her nephew, Alfred, the newly appointed footman. The arrival of this young upstart rather punctures Thomas's pleasure in his own promotion. Everyone seems to prefer Alfred and it is not long before Thomas begins to plot to find ways in which he can scupper the boy's chances in the house. The biggest problem that Thomas faces is that O'Brien has Alfred's back; and she of all people knows how best to get back at her old compatriot and has no compunction in doing so when the need arises.

So once again Thomas finds himself cast off. Rob James-Collier, the actor who plays Thomas, believes it is this theme of rejection that makes the servant so angry with the world: 'Whenever he has let someone in, he gets hurt. And it fuels his rage. So he thinks, "I'll do it all on my own."'

Robert Are you not popular downstairs?
Thomas Oh, I wouldn't say that, m'lord. But you know how people can be. They like a little joke.

Later, Thomas is petulant when he sees Carson advising Alfred on the precise uses of the many different small spoons that could be laid on the dining table. 'You never helped me,' he says. To which Carson replies, 'You never asked.' But, says James-Collier, even as a junior footman Thomas would have been shy of asking because 'He feels the world is against him. What's the point in asking? It's part of his insecurity. He doesn't want to be rejected.'

Much of Thomas's feeling of being an outsider stems from his homosexuality, or as the doctors of the time would have had it, his 'sexual inversion'. While this is not one of his defining characteristics, it is a significant aspect of his make-up and one that, in the early twentieth century, Thomas would have had to keep hidden from view. While most men of his generation were accustomed to being reticent when it came to affairs of the heart, the strain for Thomas is that he is never able to be completely himself. We must suppose that part of the appeal in staying at Downton is that it is the one place where he and his preferences are tolerated – there are hints that the rest of the household know – even if it can never be spoken of openly.

In the early twentieth century, homosexual acts were not just viewed with intolerance, they were also punishable by law. Imprisonment was known, and the widely publicised and scandalous case of Oscar Wilde (sentenced to two years' hard labour at Reading Gaol in 1895) was a memory that refused to fade – indeed, it remained the example to which everyone pointed for at least 40 years. Throughout the war there had been concerns about homosexuality amongst the troops at the Front, with so many men forced into proximity under such extreme conditions. During the course of the war, 270 soldiers and 20 officers were court-martialled for 'acts of gross indecency with another male person', according to the Guidance notes in the *Manual of Military Law*. There was very little understanding shown to the men's situation; King George V, on hearing the extent of homosexual activity in the army, is supposed to have said: 'I thought men like that shot themselves.'

At home, anxieties about homosexuality had been further raised by the alarmist – and completely unsubstantiated – articles written by the journalist and MP, Noel Pemberton Billing. He claimed that German secret agents were blackmailing '47,000 highly placed British perverts', including cabinet ministers and peers of the realm, having lured them into 'evils which all decent men thought had perished with Sodom and Lesbia'. Homosexuality, it seemed, was not merely a crime and a sin but also a threat to national security.

While those around him indulge in light-hearted flirting or make plans to leave service in order to start a family life of their own, Thomas cannot. His loneliness reveals glimmers of a softer side – such as when he sobs, wretched after the suicide of the blind officer he had grown fond of. But he is a hard-hearted man and much of his behaviour is defensive; he puts the barriers up long before anyone has a chance to get near him.

Could it be this feeling of being prejudiced against that gives rise to the more unattractive aspects of his personality? Because with Thomas it's not so much his sexuality that those around him find hard to handle, it's his malicious streak. His merciless teasing of others, his meanness to those below him in rank and dismissiveness of anybody who does not think as he does are challenging qualities to live with. He's a snob, too, flatly refusing to dress Branson when he

returns to the house as Lady Sybil's husband. The extent of Thomas's bravery must be suspected as well. He signed up for the medical corps perhaps not realising he would be exposed to such gruesome horrors of war on the front line. After he has been reminded of home – when he sees Matthew at the Front – and then frightened out of his wits when his fellow stretcher bearer is shot right beside him, Thomas decides he must get sent home. At any cost.

Having successfully accomplished his 'Blighty' (a self-inflicted wound that is not serious enough to kill but is sufficiently debilitating to get a soldier sent home from the Front), Thomas returns to England with his maimed hand. He is able to present himself as something of a wounded hero, however far from the truth this may be. He relishes his new status and also the opportunity to throw his weight around at Downton Abbey. As Acting Sergeant for the convalescent home, Thomas enjoyed a brief episode at the house not as a servant but as a man in charge, but as soon as the war ended, so too did his privileges.

Thomas If you are learning how to do your job, you should never open a shirt in a room like this where it might be marked, let alone put studs in it. Do that in a dressing room and nowhere else. Alfred Thank you.

Handsome, conceited and ambitious, Thomas is not, says Julian Fellowes, 'as clever as he thinks he is'. This misplaced self-confidence is what trips him up and thwarts his often morally dubious plans from time to time: from the occasion when the Duke of Crowborough finds and burns all the incriminating letters with which Thomas had planned to blackmail him, to when a black marketeer took everything that Thomas had ('and more besides') in exchange for inedible and therefore unsaleable goods. Carson may have been reluctant to take Thomas back into the household, but he cannot resist a man who is good at his job – and Thomas is very good at his. His pride and vanity, which are scarcely attractive qualities in themselves, did make him very exacting and able in his work as a footman. And now he is ready for a new challenge.

Thomas's new position as valet to Lord Grantham is the step up that all footmen aspired to and were trained for from the moment they entered service. It is a role that as yet eludes Molesley, who like Thomas missed the opportunity for promotion when Bates was appointed as Lord Grantham's valet in Series 1. They would be given hands-on experience when they acted as valets to any visiting guests, and in an era of large house parties this could be a taxing process. In hunting counties, of which Yorkshire was one, there were additional strains to contend with, which required not just skill but also a calm temperament. After a day following the hounds, the entire hunting party was liable to return to the house at the same moment, with all the weary hunters wanting restorative hot baths immediately. One footman at Badminton House, Gloucestershire, recalled: 'They were very free with their language, and when they'd had a bad day they vented their spleen on me. It was like water off a duck's back; one thing I learned early in service was never to allow myself to get hassled.'

Still, there were attractive perks to being a valet. It was possible, over time, to accumulate a small wardrobe of expensive 'cast-off' clothes from your master. The arrangement tended to be somewhat indirect. A man would hand over some items, whether shirts or socks, saying they could be thrown away as he had no use for them anymore. This was a kind of code. A butler at Cliveden clarified matters to a bemused footman, who was surprised to be given those instructions with a handful of apparently brand-new silk ties. He explained, 'This is the way gentlemen of breeding offer you their old clothes as a present.' The footman was not supposed to throw them away, but to keep them for himself.

Being in a position of trust could also offer opportunities for those who were prepared to bend the rules. The rather oblique approach to 'giving' adopted by many gentlemen encouraged some valets to adopt an equally oblique approach to taking. One valet recalled that he 'began "accidentally" to leave the odd thing out when I was packing a case at the end of a stay until I had a tidy collection of shirts, vests, underpants and socks'. Sometimes items might be 'loaned' rather than taken. If a gentlemen changed his clothes twice a day and bathed regularly, as was the norm, the valet might wear the cast-off clothes for a couple of days before putting them into the laundry. Care had to be taken not to be too conspicuous, particularly as a family crest or initials may be sewn onto certain items. One footman was sacked when he was caught wearing a house guest's socks.

Thomas's working day as a valet is rather less onerous than when he was a footman, at least from the point of view of running up and down the back stairs all the time. His principal role is to make sure that Lord Grantham is properly

turned out at all times, whether at Downton, in London or elsewhere. Thomas is expected to travel with him, wherever he goes, but in any place the framework for the day remains the same. The day begins with Thomas taking up a 'calling tray' with tea on it, before brushing and laying out his lordship's clothes for the day. He then takes charge of the dressing room and bedroom, making sure that the fires are lit and the rooms dusted and cleaned by the housemaids, and removing any clothes that need to be cleaned or mended. Unlike the women, Lord Grantham would remain in the same clothes until it was time to change for dinner, when Thomas helps him to dress. During the day, Thomas must be on hand at all times to assist if his master decides to go for a walk and so needs his hat, coat, gloves, boots and walking cane. If Lord Grantham intends to go away, Thomas is responsible for packing the correct attire. Any mending or spot-cleaning would also be done by the valet.

However, over time a valet would – or could – become much more than a mere clothes' brusher and tray-carrier. As Ernest King recalled in his memoir, *The Green Baize Door*, a good valet might be 'depended on to do everything and forget nothing'. He would not need to be told what to pack for a journey, he would 'know': 'He should be prepared to dress his man for a funeral or a fancy-dress ball. He must never be caught napping, he must be able to produce everything, even shoes so well polished they may be used as a mirror in an emergency!'

To bring Thomas to life, James-Collier first had to tone down all of his movements. 'Normally I gesture a lot when I talk. But back then, everything was much more restrained. I've had to change my walk. In Series 1, there is a scene when I walk into a library. Now I look at it and think, that's all wrong. Too much movement. A perfect footman was like a racehorse. He had been trained for years to perform all these tasks. It is almost balletic: you have to be quick but discreet in everything that you do.'

Thomas's time as Acting Sergeant in the house, which set him apart from the servants, as well as working alongside Lady Sybil when she was a nurse for the convalescing officers, might have muddied the divide between above stairs and below for him, but Thomas doesn't seek to refashion the world order; he is only interested in improving his place within it. While he may respect Lady Sybil more, having worked alongside her with the convalescing officers, it doesn't sit easily with him that she ran off with the chauffeur. No, it is not that Thomas seeks to refashion the world order, but to be master of his own domain – even if that domain is only Lord Grantham's dressing room and the servants' hall.

Different collars were worn for different occasions. Although in general the collar had become softer, lower and more comfortable since Edwardian times, for formal occasions Thomas would still make sure that Lord Grantham was fitted out with a wing collar – a so-called 'tipped imperial' or 'Gladstone'.

MRS ISIDORE LEVINSON

MOTHER OF THE
COUNTESS OF GRANTHAM

Of the two main transatlantic carriers, the Cunard Line offered speed while the White Star Line provided luxurious comfort, so it is no surprise that Martha should have chosen to travel with the latter. White Star's three 'Olympic Class' liners – *Titanic*, *Britannic* and *Olympic* – created just before the First World War, were amongst the largest and most splendid ever built, featuring grand staircases, panelled salons and en suites in first-class cabins. The *Titanic*, of course, sank on her maiden voyage in 1912 and *Britannic* (converted into a hospital ship during the war) was sunk by a German mine in 1916, but *Olympic* – sumptuously refitted immediately after the war – continued to cross the Atlantic until the 1930s.

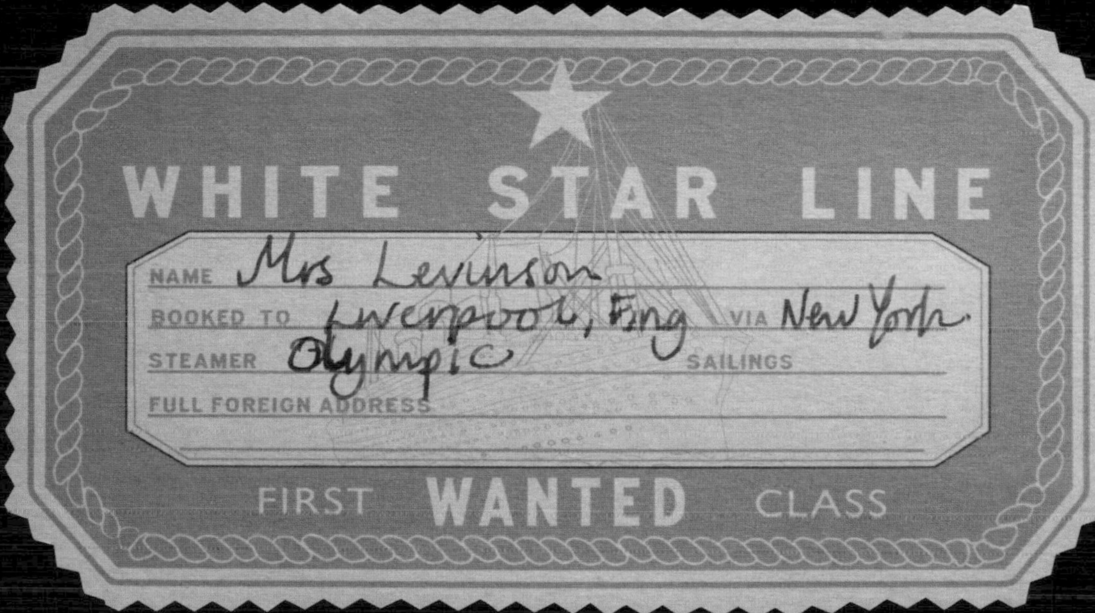

WHITE STAR LINE

NAME Mrs Levinson
BOOKED TO Liverpool, Eng VIA New York
STEAMER Olympic SAILINGS
FULL FOREIGN ADDRESS

FIRST WANTED CLASS

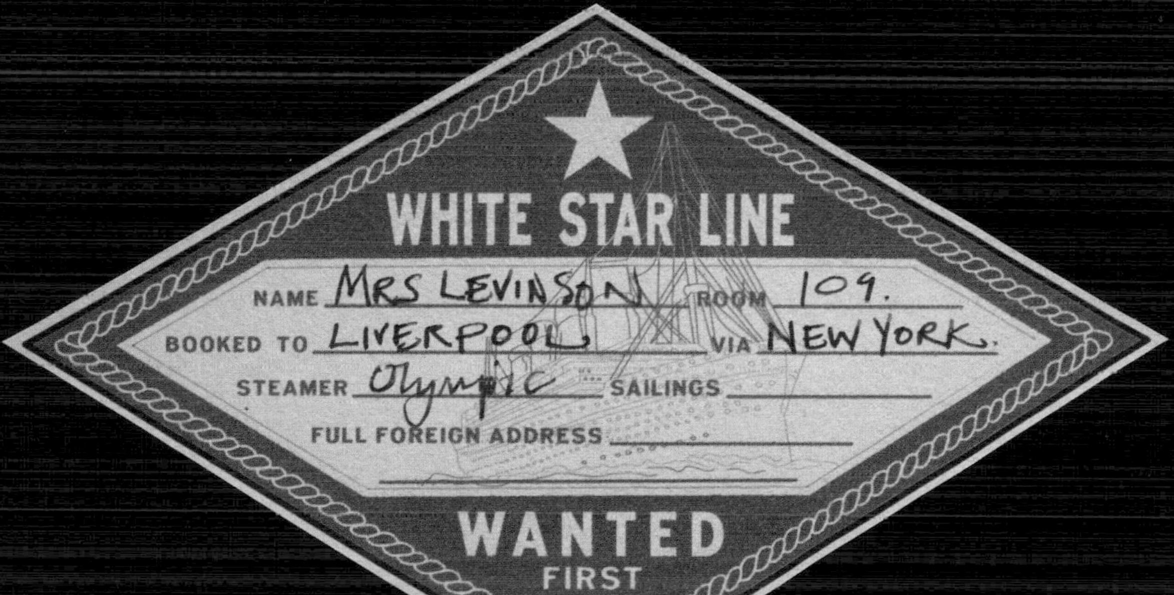

WHITE STAR LINE

NAME MRS LEVINSON ROOM 109.
BOOKED TO LIVERPOOL VIA NEW YORK.
STEAMER Olympic SAILINGS
FULL FOREIGN ADDRESS

WANTED
FIRST
CLASS

Martha Carson. Mrs Hughes. The world has moved on since last we met.

Carson And we've moved on with it, Madam.

Martha Really? It seems strange to think of the English embracing change ...

Martha is rich. However impressed we have been by the Crawleys' wealth – with their castle and vast estate, legacy of fine art and furniture, properties up and down the country from London to Scotland and the leisured life of the family, not to mention the large number of servants who attend to their every need – this is all as nothing compared to the riches of Cora's American family.

The scale of American fortunes after the First World War was out of all proportion to those of the wealthy British, and Martha wears the weight of it well. Comfortable with her financial status, confident in who she is and happy to enjoy the lavish luxuries that all her money can bring her, Martha enters Downton Abbey with suitable aplomb.

There is a certain nervousness ahead of Martha's arrival – Violet, for one, is none too keen on her opposite number. In talking to Isobel Crawley, it is revealed that while Martha's husband was Jewish, she herself is not, and their children were raised as Episcopalians. As Julian Fellowes explains, this was normal practice: 'He didn't convert but allowed his children to be brought up as non-Jewish for ease of life. This was quite usual then.' Isobel remarks that it must have been due to the prejudices of Wall Street that the Levinson family made this move and commends Violet for her broad view. Violet does not take the compliment: 'She was American. That was quite enough to be going on with.'

Even Martha's own daughter does not seem entirely comfortable around her. Cora is not exactly cowed by her mother, but nor does she assert herself. They do correspond frequently, and it appears that Martha has always been

content with the marriage her daughter made. Cora, for her part, is defensive of her mother's right to hold onto her own money – having rescued Downton once. Now that Robert has lost the money she sees no reason why Martha should be expected to bail out the Crawleys again.

Cora You don't have to give money after every conversation, Mather...

Martha No? Isn't that what the English expect of rich Americans?

Mary thinks differently: to her, the saving of an ancient English estate is a matter of almost moral importance – certainly she believes it is a more worthy investment of the Levinson money than the ideas of her playboy uncle, who apparently intends to spend his share of the inheritance on fast yachts and women. It is Edith who brings out the best in Martha; her desire to get married and live happily ever after is one that her grandmother understands, and together they gang up on Robert to try and make this happen. Robert, of course, is quite defenceless in the face of his determined mother-in-law. Besides which Robert must still feel indebted to her for the sizeable dowry she bestowed on him upon his marriage to her daughter – a fortune that he has now lost.

Shirley MacLaine, the legendary Hollywood actress, has joined the cast for the third series to play Martha, and she was, according to Liz Trubridge, producer, 'tickled by the idea of it'. MacLaine believes that her character's attitude comes not so much from her money as her politics: 'Her confidence comes from being a democratic American – she is so centred in her fairness and considers America to be fair, and tradition is not fair.' Martha is driven by a desire to convert the rest of the world to democracy, and with this mission in mind she loses no time in telling everyone what they ought to be doing and how they ought to be doing it. 'She has watched a war from overseas and doesn't want it to happen to them again. But she approaches it from an intellectual standpoint,' says MacLaine. 'She's still impressed by the aristocracy but more impressed with the notion of changing their attitudes.'

Martha Dearest Mary, now you tell me all of your wedding plans and I'll see what I can do to improve them.

While she may have once been awed by the English upper classes (this, after all, was why she brought her daughter over to be presented at the London Season), she welcomes the post-war changes that are being brought to England, even if they seem slower in coming to Downton Abbey. As Gareth Neame explains, 'When Julian created the role of Cora, not much thought was given to her family other than how it informed her back story. On reaching Series 3, it seems likely the girls' grandmother might visit on occasion, and we liked the idea of the moneyed new world colliding with the order of the old. At Downton we see the modern world shaking things up and how the various characters respond to that change is part of the fun. Martha is a big part of this modern intrusion.'

Back home in Newport, Rhode Island (a fashionable, smart state), arriving in an outsized Cadillac would be *de rigueur* amongst her set. There, she would not even be amongst the richest. There were American billionaires such as Henry Ford, John D. Rockefeller Jr and Andrew Mellon, and multi-multi-millionaires such as the Vanderbilts (whose daughter married the Duke of Marlborough and rescued the seat), the Astors, Andrew Carnegie and J. P. Morgan. But even American millionaires, such as Martha and her late husband, tended to have more millions than all but the richest of British grandees and plutocrats. This divide was only going to get bigger. American industry was in a good position in 1920; having not had to devote all its industrial efforts and manpower to the war effort as its European counterparts had, it was ready to exploit the opportunities to export to Europe in peacetime. Martha was able to hire an American car on arrival in England because of the recent big influx of them at a time when the British motor industry was struggling to get back on its feet. (Although only the chassis would have been shipped over from the States; the body work would have been made in Britain.)

Furthermore, while the New Rich in England tended to be sneered at by the Old Rich (or Not Rich Anymore) as they bought their way into the Establishment – purchasing titles and land, attempting to portray themselves as old families with heritage and class – the Americans had an unabashed belief that their money made them important and gave them a position in Society, too. They displayed their wealth and it gave them confidence.

Martha Nothing ever alters for you people, does it? Revolutions erupt and monarchies crash to the ground, and the groom still cannot see the bride before the wedding.

Americans were buoyed up by the knowledge that the European monarchies were falling. The Republican path seemed to be the modern, relevant choice. The Russian Revolution and the brutal killing of Tsar Nicholas II and his family had led to the emergence of a stronger Socialist movement well beyond Russia's own borders. The Tsar had been a first cousin and good friend of King George V, but they had been forced apart by the war. Even when the King knew his dear relative and immediate family urgently needed shelter from the revolutionaries in 1917, he thought it wiser to withdraw the British Government's offer of giving them asylum (the murders happened the following year). There was a very real fear that the same revolution could come to Britain. As a precaution, the King changed the name of the Royal House from the House of Saxe-Coburg to the House of Windsor, in an attempt to distance the family from its close Teutonic cousins. During the war and in the years after, the monarchies of Austria, Germany, Greece and Spain also fell; many of the ex-rulers of these countries were relatives of the King. Extraordinarily enough, thanks to the resilience and tactical moves of George V and Queen Mary (whose father was of German extraction), the British royal family's popularity actually grew during this time. But it was touch and go. To the observing Americans, it must have seemed as if the British aristocracy was just one domino in the line, waiting for its turn to tumble.

Still, even at this time, many wealthy Americans had strong Anglophile tendencies, together with an admiration for the British upper classes and their way of life. After all, they married off many of their daughters into the British aristocracy. A few American families, most notably the Astors, actually settled in England, acquired land, were ennobled and became part of the British elite. Most, however, preferred to create something of the aristocratic way of life back home, hoping to import the class for themselves. Liveried footmen became a popular adornment at grand New York dinner parties, as the English

servants were thought to bring tone and expertise, two things the newly rich lacked. They were, in the words of one American commentator, 'the expensive, smooth-running, imported mechanism without which the social race could not be run'.

Amongst the Stateside millionaires there was a particular vogue for English butlers. What the East Coast rich really valued, according to P. G. Wodehouse, were 'butlers who weighed 250 pounds on the hoof, butlers with three chins and bulging abdomens, butlers with large gooseberry eyes and that austere butlerine manner which has passed so completely away'. Carson must have been anxious that Martha might make a bid for him.

In fact, Martha is completely convinced by the American way, preferring to have her young lady's maid, Reed, who she can train up to her requirements, rather than an old-fashioned English servant looking at her askance. Her attitude is unnerving to some, but it was just part of what the aristocracy thought of as the more generally unsettling Americanisation of British life. It was an almost constant theme in the press; during 1920 *The Lady* magazine contained several articles about the arrival of American words ('chore' was singled out) and jazz.

Reed, too, unnerves the servants below stairs, particularly Alfred and Daisy. She takes a shine to Alfred, who is taken aback by her advances (no English girl would have even thought of making the first move), even if he does rather like it. Daisy is put out by Reed's forward manner, but she is prompted to wonder if there's something in this modern attitude that she should be adopting too. Even Daisy, deep in the bowels of the kitchen, would be feeling the increasing influence of Hollywood films and their romantic storylines, the starlets who came from nowhere (Clara Bow, the original 'It Girl', was born in a slum tenement) and the magazines that wrote endlessly of their love affairs and style.

Violet It's so encouraging to see the future unfurl.

Martha As long as you remember it will bear no resemblance to the past.

It is not just Martha who ruffles the feathers of the British at Downton; her maid, Reed, causes quite a stir amongst the servants with her forward American manner.

Naturally, Martha looks the part of an American millionaire. Caroline McCall flew out to Los Angeles to do the fitting with Shirley MacLaine. 'Usually, when you are dressing someone of a certain age you backdate them,' explains McCall. 'Most people find a style in their forties and stick with it, but Martha is so wealthy she adopts new fashions as they come out.' Unlike Violet, who still looks like Queen Alexandra in her S-bend corset, Martha has the new waistless shift shape, to show what a modern woman she is. 'She's very showy, happy to display her riches. There's always a lot of big jewellery. She wears bandeau headdresses, or hats with expensive feathers – one of them has birds-of-paradise feathers in it. The American clothes of that period were much fussier in terms of decoration than European ones,' says McCall. 'They hadn't worked out that less is more. Plus, we wanted Martha to look as if she had arrived from another planet.'

Despite her zeal, Martha will find that her mission to change the family's attitudes and modernise their politics is not without its obstacles – not least because they are unaccustomed to the rather forthright manner she adopts in such discussions. The Crawleys are rather more used to tip-toeing their way around any issues that might cause upheaval, from sex to money and religion, but Martha will always wade right in.

Martha Are there still forbidden subjects? In 1920? I can't believe it.

But as exhausting as some members of the household, such as Violet and Carson, find Martha's determination to shake things up a bit, the others may reluctantly admit that there is something in what she says, after all. It remains to be seen whether her way will win out in the end.

From dieting to body building, Americans embraced health and fitness fads after the First World War. 'Reducing' – or losing weight – became a major concern, for both health and fashion reasons. (The 'smoking diet' was one popular regime!) Americans, along with the French, made 'sunbathing' fashionable. John Harvey Kellogg (the inventor of Corn Flakes) was convinced of the healthful properties of sunlight on skin and advocated the 'healthy tan'. Expatriate Americans created a sensation on the French Riviera by lying out on the beach.

MR JOHN BATES

FORMER VALET TO THE
EARL OF GRANTHAM

LIFE PRISONER

Mary Anderson
145 Offington Rd S.W.   Paddington 904

Mrs K. Adams
14 Eaton Rd S.W.   Victoria 4102

Miss. E. Ainley
51 London Rd S.E.

Mr. P. Ackroyd
23 Higginson Place   City 4560
E.1.

Mrs. A. Bartlett
14 Crannount Street S.E.

P. Barking
25 Regents Place. W.   Ealing 1574

Mr. N. Bonville
53 Victoria Street, Yorkshire.

Anna transcribed the names of friends of the original Mr and Mrs Bates from his first wife's address book, hoping to talk to them to garner evidence to support his appeal. Often, attention to detail, and sifting through an apparently innocuous mass of information, was the key to unlocking a mystery – a tactic Anna would have discovered from the ever-growing selection of literature on crime and detection available at the time, including Agatha Christie's first Poirot novel, *The Mysterious Affair at Styles*, published in 1920.

Mrs. C. Church
16 Grove Terrace N.W.

P. Corkdale   Battersea
35 Trinity Cottages   904
    Andrew Street S.W

Frankie Darcy
16 Pickering Street
    Cork, Ireland.

Mr. J. L Flanaghan   Museum
47 New Street

Mr. A O'Flaherty   Dublin
59 Upper Oldfield Pk. 3021
    Clontarf

Mr. Harlip
16 Station Road
    Cromleigh, Lancashire

Bates It's the stuff of my dreams. The panic that a dinner won't be ready, or that a frock isn't ironed, or a gun wasn't cleaned.

As the new year dawns, bringing hope to those ready to leave the horrors of wartime behind and make a fresh start, the residents of Downton Abbey are poised to embrace the new decade with optimism. Almost all are ready, that is, but for one of their number. Bates, valet to the Earl of Grantham, husband of Anna and friend of almost all the other servants and the Crawley family, is locked in a prison cell, convicted of his first wife's murder. Bates is hoping to appeal against his conviction, but until that can happen he must reconcile himself to prison life. He is in for a long stretch, 20 years at least; though this is better than it might have been – at his trial he was sentenced to be hanged.

Living under the threat of death for some weeks until his reprieve was obtained would have been enormously traumatic for Bates. At least, we must imagine that it was. Bates is a man who has been so opaque and guarded in his emotions that even those closest to him have had to patiently and slowly tease out details about his past. So his present mental state is something that we – and those around him – can only guess at. What might be taken for silent strength could perhaps mask a fragile temperament. Bates has admitted that when he was invalided out of the army after the Boer War he felt lost and became a drunkard. He believed then that he had made his wife's life such a misery that he needed to atone by going to prison for a crime that she had committed. He has not always, in other words, been a man able to take whatever life threw at him with an upright, stiff-upper-lip attitude. Beneath that calm exterior we know there is a man who is kind and sensitive to the feelings of those close to him, and that is why he is one of the most loved characters in the series.

Meeting Anna changed everything for Bates. When he began working at Downton Abbey, his one hope had been to hold onto his job – something that, at times, looked highly unlikely. The other servants were at best doubtful that he would be able to do the work demanded of him because of his limp and walking stick, and at worst they plotted to get him the sack. Bates fought to keep his position. It provided a refuge and it kept him apart from his now estranged wife, Vera. Having a criminal record, he knew that other work opportunities would be extremely limited. At Downton he had a roof over his head, three meals a day and the patronage of his friend and master, Lord Grantham. Despite his rather enigmatic manner, Bates's fundamental goodness and fairness to all shone through and it wasn't long before he had won the respect of nearly all the staff below stairs.

Unexpectedly, he fell in love with Anna and she returned his feelings, giving him the chance to dream again of a happy future, and together they planned a family life, running a small country hotel. At this moment, in prison, just one thing will be keeping him going and that is the faith that Anna, now his wife, has in him. She loves him, absolutely and entirely, and knowing that gives him the strength he needs to get through the long years in prison he believes lie ahead. As Brendan Coyle, the actor who plays Bates, says: 'At first he doesn't think he's worthy of Anna – of this goodness that's come into his life. She frees him from himself, and allows him to express himself more. He comes to feel that he is worthy of her.'

Thwarted once again in their desire to be together, those years in prison will be long indeed. Having been through a relatively brief spell in prison before, when he took the rap for Vera's theft of the regimental silver, he knows what he's in for. But it's one thing to nobly serve a sentence on someone else's behalf, knowing that your crime would be considered quite petty and that there's a date not too far away when you will get out again, and quite another to be staring at many long years of confinement and hard labour as a convicted murderer.

Bates Don't you understand? While I'm in here, you have to live my life as well as your own.

Bates is respected by most of his fellow servants and the Crawley family, which was proven through the support they gave him in court.

Nor should we underestimate what he has been through up to this point. His experiences in the Boer War would have been intense and difficult ('It was a horrific conflict,' says Coyle, 'a guerrilla war'); extraordinary enough for him to forge a friendship with Lord Grantham, to whom he was a soldier-servant. Bates suffered immense disappointment that his career was over, after he was forced out of the army because of an injury that left him, as a relatively young man, dependent upon a walking stick. He might otherwise, believes Julian Fellowes, have enjoyed a long and successful military career. On top of which, on his return, his former wife – whom he once loved – turned into a bitter and shrill harridan, intent on making his every moment wretched. For a decent man of moral virtue, he must have felt that he had taken quite enough punishment even before his incarceration began.

On entering prison, newly convicted prisoners faced a dehumanisation process. Bates would not be referred to by name but by his assigned number, and while interned he must wear an ill-fitting suit with few home comforts permitted. The environment itself is harsh, too. Like many others across the country, Bates's prison is a purpose-built Victorian edifice. Within it, tiers of echoing galleries radiate from a central observation core, with long rows of tiny cells, each one sealed shut with a heavy iron door, adding to the overwhelming atmosphere of grim oppression.

Bates's sentence would have begun with a 12-week period of 'lone confinement', when the prisoner was supposed to ponder his crimes. One convict at the time described the hell: 'Prisoners generally suffered a reaction after conviction, and frequently had nervous breakdowns. There was a great danger of suicide and incipient madness during the early period of separate confinement. There was nothing to relieve the strain except two educational books, a Bible and a prayer book.'

The conditions in which prisoners lived were usually spartan; cells tended to be narrow, 10 by 7 feet, and perhaps 9 feet high, containing little but a bed board (made of two planks), a table, a stool and a shelf for the small number of books and a few personal possessions they would be allowed to keep. The air was stale, the lighting poor, and in the winter months it would be bitterly cold.

As a 'lifer', Bates is entitled to certain rewards and privileges, as it was thought then that the punitive elements of prison ceased to be effective over prolonged periods and it was better to ameliorate prisoners' conditions – although this process was both relative and gradual. Bates could, for one, receive more letters and have longer visits – 30 minutes, as opposed to the regulation 20 – which

Anna I do not believe when Vera decided
to kill herself she never mentioned it to
another living soul.

would mean a great deal to him and to Anna. He would also be allowed to earn 1d a day to spend on 'comforts' – biscuits, pickles, jam and sugar (but not tobacco). These items may sound modest but they were extremely welcome, as prison food was meagre and disgusting. Manny Shinwell, imprisoned for political insurrection in 1919, never forgot the horror of his first prison breakfast: 'I was handed a large stone jar of the kind that holds jam or marmalade. It was nearly full of a greyish-looking thickened liquid which I presumed was called porridge – a description that would have made any Scots-born official in the place rise in wrath. Along with it came a small canister of milk. As soon as the door closed I tried the milk. It was sour.' He found himself quite unable to eat or drink a single drop. The midday meal was a jar of similarly indigestible 'soup'. Shinwell survived his five-month sentence solely on tea and bread.

Anna How are you getting on with your new companion?

Bates I don't like him, but, so far, I've kept it to myself ...

Grim as the food was, the grinding tedium of the daily routine was far worse. Roused at 6.30 each morning, inmates would work in their cells for a few hours, sewing nosebags or mailbags, with short releases to attend a service in the chapel and to take an hour's walk in the prison yard. This exercise was vividly described by one prison reformer as 'a monotonous and uninterrupted perambulation in single file round and round two concentric tracks under the orders and vigilant gaze of warders'. Nor were they allowed to talk to each other, although all convicts learned to talk without moving their lips so as to subvert this rule. The afternoons would be spent continuing their labours in workshops, again in silence and under the watchful eye of the prison officers. Lunch and tea (bread and cocoa) would be taken alone in their cells, the latter at 4.15pm, signalling the long watch of the night. Prisoners were left alone in their cells for some 15 hours until the monotonous routine began again the following morning.

Weekends, far from being a period of respite, were worse. Prisoners spent from noon on Saturday until Monday morning in their cells, with only three brief breaks – two chapel services on Sunday and a half-hour's exercise session.

The boredom was soul destroying – small wonder Bates seizes upon even seemingly trivial chit-chat with Anna. She thinks that with all the worry over proving his innocence he can't possibly be interested in the plans for Lady Mary's wedding or the minor dramas of the kitchens. She couldn't be more wrong.

For relief from the tedium, Bates would relish anything novel – the weekly bath was a highlight for prisoners, together with the weekly change of clothes. Recent reforms did mean that some prisons had lectures and cultural events, even the occasional film screening. But an educated and reflective inmate such as Bates would be most likely to borrow books from the library. Given his need to escape from the seriousness of his concerns, he might have enjoyed the work of P. G. Wodehouse. Jeeves, a valet like him, had made his first appearance in a short story published in 1915, with his character developing in further collections. Or Bates might pick up Wodehouse's *Something Fresh*, which featured Blandings Castle, a setting not dissimilar to Downton Abbey in many ways. Reading about the frustrations of chinless aristocrats, forced to ask their always far superior servants how to replace a stolen policeman's hat or some other minor caper, would no doubt have given Bates a much-needed chuckle.

More worrying than the problem of how to survive the boredom was the constant threat of violence, felt in every prison, from both the warders and fellow inmates. Discipline could appear arbitrary. Small offences might be punished with solitary confinement, or a restriction of privileges. The Penal Reform League, having compiled reports from former convicts, came to the conclusion that the warders were often 'tyrannical bullies' who gained promotion by cowing the prisoners. One convict, imprisoned in 1919, characterised the prison officers or 'screws' as of four different types: 'There were the slackers, the sneaks, the bullies and the officious. They were much divided into cliques. Some of them indulged in filthy jests and were of a low mental type. Some of them were corrupt.'

All of this will present Bates with a battle to hold onto his sense of self – he has almost no control over his own life anymore and the overpowering feeling of helplessness meant that many others like him lost the fight. Bates, with his military background and schooling in the life of service, is better equipped than most to deal with the ennui of prison. There are flashes of temper, too, that we have seen in the past – that chink in his armour that led him to reach for the bottle before. It will stand him in good stead now if he needs to defend himself, but as anyone knows, if you use a weapon – whether anger, fists or a knife – you must be prepared to have the same used against you. Bates's greatest danger may in fact be himself, as he struggles to survive for as long as it takes to prove his innocence.

The comforts of prison life were few. Bates, in his cell, had a narrow shelf on which he could place standard-issue books and a small selection of personal possessions. The photograph of Anna was the most important for Bates, reminding him of life beyond the prison walls.

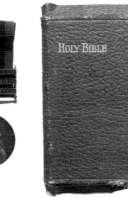

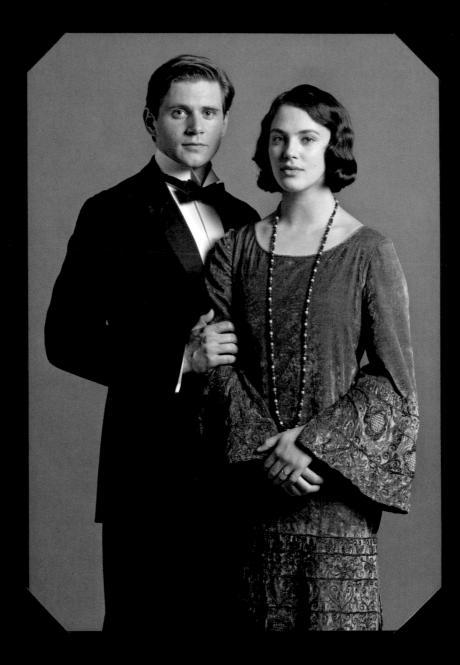

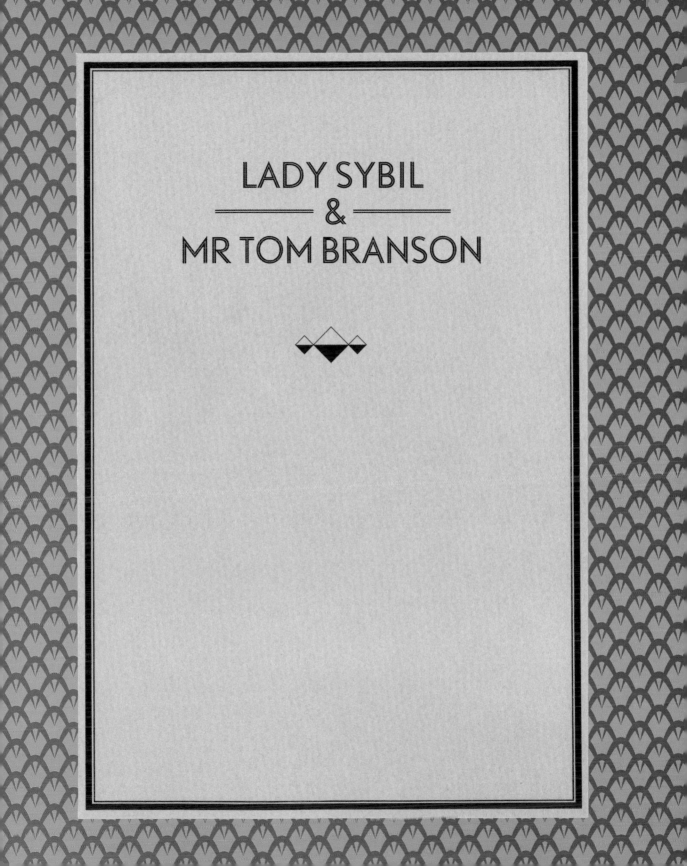

LADY SYBIL
&
MR TOM BRANSON

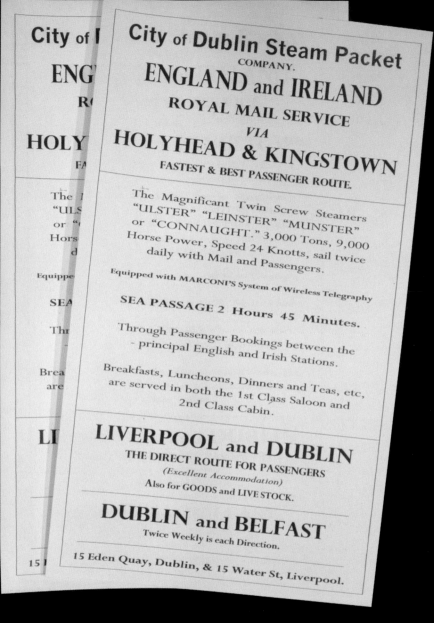

Returning home to Downton Abbey was a far speedier exercise for Lady Sybil and Tom Branson in 1920, if they used the fast and regular steamboat service between Dublin and Liverpool. The City of Dublin Steam Packet Company was the oldest established carrier, having been founded in 1822. Its four large, twin-screw steam ships, built in 1897, could reach speeds of 24 knots. Unfortunately, two of these magnificent ships – the *Connaught* and the *Leinster* – were sunk by German torpedoes during the war.

THE CITY OF DUBLIN STEAM PACKET COMPANY'S VESSELS.

The Magnificent Twin Screw Steamers "ULSTER" "LEINSTER" "MUNSTER" or "CONNAUGHT."

TO DUBLIN AND LIVERPOOL.

DURING THE MONTH OF MAY, 1920, AS FOLLOWS

Leaves Dublin	Leaves Liverpool
6:45 a.m.	7:15 a.m.
8:00 a.m.	8:45 a.m.
9:30 a.m.	10:15 a.m.
11:00 a.m.	11:45 a.m.
12:30 a.m.	1:15 p.m.
2:00 p.m.	2:45 p.m.
3:45 p.m.	4:30 p.m.
5:15 p.m.	6:00 p.m.
7:00 p.m.	7:45 p.m.
8:30 p.m.	9:30 p.m.
10:30 p.m.	11:30 p.m.
12:15 a.m.	1:05 a.m.

SUNDAYS AND BANK HOLIDAYS

No Trips at 6:45 a.m. or 7:15 a.m.

Information as to rates of Freights, Fares, etc, will be given by the Agents of the Company.

15 Eden Quay, Dublin, & 15 Water St, Liverpool.

Isobel He's making a problem where none exists. No one could care less were Branson at the wedding or not.

Matthew You must think country life more exciting than it is, if you imagine people don't care when an earl's daughter runs off with a chauffeur.

On the face of it, the young newlyweds Sybil and Tom hope to live an unobtrusive, quiet existence in Dublin as 'Mr and Mrs Branson', happily waiting for the arrival of their baby. Tom is pursuing a new career as a journalist, writing for the radical nationalist newspapers, and Sybil is looking to work as a nurse once the baby is born, busying herself with managing their little flat and cooking her husband's suppers in the meantime. But as the gossip back at Downton Abbey shows, nothing of their way of life is normal. An earl's daughter and a chauffeur-turned-Irish-revolutionary cannot expect an uneventful life together. And perhaps it is disingenuous of the two of them to think that they can.

Sybil, after all, has worked as a nurse in wartime and this has changed her outlook forever; she wants to live life differently and on her own terms. She has always embraced opportunities to excite change (remember her outlandish, trousered outfit designed to shock, not to mention her attendance at political rallies?) and running off with a firebrand chauffeur is another. As Julian Fellowes says, 'I'm sure plenty of people were attracted to each other across the barriers. But I think Sybil is essentially a rebel. And one of her ways of expressing her rebellion is Branson. It isn't only that she finds him attractive or is in love with him. It suits her to have a statement of rebellion in her life choice.'

Sybil might challenge this view – she likes to believe that love is what motivates her – but she wouldn't deny that after the war she no longer believes that society can pick up and carry on as it was before. Nor, having exposed herself to great suffering and trauma and having seen for herself how all men are equal in

the face of tragedy, would she want it to. Sybil believes there is no reason why her marriage to Tom should not work – she doesn't see the differences in their background as relevant, let alone affecting their chances of a contented life together.

For Tom it's more complicated. Ardently left wing, anti-establishment, increasingly anti-English and getting deeper into the Irish nationalist movement, his falling in love with an earl's daughter would be harder to explain back home, but for the fact that he can point to the zealous attitude they both share to change the world. 'They are by far the most forward-thinking couple,' says Allen Leech, the actor playing Tom. 'They have a shared spark and that's what attracts them. Sybil has always enjoyed putting the cat amongst the pigeons, ever since she came downstairs in that outfit. And Branson loves that.'

But where Sybil's politics were either harmless (the right to wear trousers) or a force for good (particularly her defiance of her mother to work as a nurse), Tom's can be more dangerous. Dublin in 1920 was almost a war zone. For anyone living in the city at that time life was dangerous, but for a revolutionary republican it was even more fraught with peril. And it was scarcely any less risky for Sybil, who – as an upper-class Englishwoman – could have become a target for attack.

The situation had deep roots. Many Irish people (particularly in the southern and western counties) had long campaigned to have a greater say in the running of their own affairs. Initially it had been envisioned that this devolution could occur within the framework of the United Kingdom – with Ireland having its own assembly for debating local questions, while continuing to send MPs to Westminster to contribute to broader national and international debates. In the late nineteenth century, two attempts to introduce such 'Home Rule' were tried, but both were thwarted by the House of Lords, which vetoed the bill after it was passed in the Commons. Finally, in 1914, after the powers of the House of Lords were curtailed, an Irish Home Rule bill was passed. But the outbreak of the First World War delayed its implementation – it was decided that the need to present a united front against the enemy was more important. Some sections within the Irish nationalist movement balked at this delay and, at Easter 1916, they tried to force the pace, by beginning an armed rising against British rule in Dublin. This Easter Rising had limited popular support, and was speedily put down.

But the execution of the Rising's leaders provoked a great deal of anger in Ireland, and led to a huge increase in support for their aims and ideals. Further anti-British sentiment was stirred up in 1918 when (due to the urgent need for troops) it was suggested that the Irish might be conscripted into the British Army. By the end of the war the nature of Irish nationalism had changed decisively, hardening into a desire not just for Home Rule, but for actual independence. In the 1918 General Election, Sinn Fein, the radical political party that expressed this new nationalism, won 73 of the 105 Irish seats. The newly elected MPs (including one female candidate, the Countess Markewicz) refused to take their places in the House of Commons at Westminster, declining to take an oath of allegiance to the British Crown. Instead, they assembled in Dublin and made a unilateral declaration of Irish Independence. They formed themselves into the Dáil, and claimed to represent the new Republic of Ireland.

Lloyd George's recently formed coalition government refused to recognise this arrangement, and instead put forward a new Home Rule bill, superceding the 1914 one that had never been implemented. The Better Government of Ireland Bill – offering considerable devolution – was introduced into Parliament in December 1919. It is this bill (which was finally passed in November 1920) that is discussed throughout the third series.

Isobel Do you approve of the new Act?

Branson Would you approve if your country had been divided by a foreign power?

The Dáil, however, refused to countenance the proposal, and instead declared a War of Independence against the British. From January 1919, across southern Ireland, violent incidents began to multiply as the Irish Republican Army (IRA) launched a campaign of terror against all aspects of British rule. The principal target was the Royal Irish Constabulary (RIC), but anyone or anything who represented or embodied British authority became a target. The British retaliated to this provocation – often with extreme savagery. In September 1919 Britain declared both the Dáil and Sinn Fein illegal.

There were several incidents in Dublin: an attempted assassination of a British general as he drove through Phoenix Park, attacks on RIC barracks, strikes by Irish workers refusing to aid the British war effort. A resident magistrate was hauled off a South Dublin tram and shot three times in the head. In February 1920, Dublin and six other southern Irish counties were declared as being in a 'state of disturbance'. It would have been very frightening for Robert

Sybil I just want to make things easier for you.

Branson For me or for you? Don't disappoint me, Sybil. Not now that we're here.

and Cora to read of such things in the paper, and think of their daughter caught up in such troubled times. 'Big Houses' (the mansions of the old Protestant land-owning aristocracy of Ireland) also began to be attacked and burnt – as symbols of British imperial oppression. Thirty such properties were torched in 1920, and many more in the years that followed.

From early in 1920, the RIC began to be reinforced from the UK by 'Auxis' (Auxillaries – ex-British Army officers) and Temporary Constables (known as 'Black and Tans' on account of their motley khaki uniforms) as well as by the British Army itself. Numerous acts of brutality against civilians were carried out – especially by the Black and Tans: whole villages were burnt, suspects were executed. These actions only fuelled anti-British feeling.

Branson Those places are different for me. I don't look at them and see charm and gracious living. I see something horrible.

Dublin by the end of 1920 was not a safe place to be. Michael Collins, the leader of the IRA in the city, aimed to launch three attacks a day. Policemen and soldiers were ambushed and killed, officials were assassinated in their offices. The tit-for-tat atrocities reached a peak on 21 November when the IRA attempted to wipe out 19 British Intelligence operatives in Dublin, in a series of early-morning raids. They killed 14 of them. In response, a party of Auxillaries drove into the Dublin stadium, Croke Park, during a Gaelic football match and opened fire on the crowd; 14 people were killed and 65 injured. The day became known as 'Bloody Sunday'. (Events escalated until July 1921, when a truce was declared. A treaty was negotiated, giving southern Ireland independence within the Commonwealth. It was generally accepted, though some hard-liners within the nationalist movement refused to consent and launched a civil war against their former comrades. The anti-treaty side eventually lost in 1923.)

It is against this violent backdrop that Sybil and Tom return to Downton. It is hardly surprising that some of the Crawley family find it difficult to welcome Tom to their bosom. Knowing the fear Sybil must be living in, they must also contend with the fact that their son-in-law shares nothing of their beliefs or way of doing things. This leaves Tom in a defensive position: torn between wanting to do the right thing by the woman he loves and his loyalty to his political ideals.

On top of which, he is emasculated by his inability to provide for her. Unhappily for him, his journalism pays only a meagre wage, when it pays at all; most of the time they are living off the allowance Sybil receives from her father. So there is no feeling for him of being able to take his bride back to her family home with him as her provider. He is unable to plant himself with both feet above stairs as, say, Mary's former suitor, Sir Richard Carlisle could – he, too, might be unschooled in aristocratic ways but his money and confidence meant he could ride over any bumps. And besides, Tom still feels the pull of belonging below stairs – not just because they were once his colleagues and friends, but because as a revolutionary he is supposed to be fighting for equality and against the rule of the aristocracy. To allow himself to be dressed for dinner by a footman makes a mockery of his beliefs. As Leech puts it: 'It's a huge issue for him, that he can't provide for his family. The fact that he's living off the very thing that he's fighting against is very difficult for him. It is an embarrassment. And it can make him touchy.' As Sybil tells Mary: 'He puts a tough face on it and says things that make everyone angry, but he so wants your good opinion. I can't tell you how much.'

Nor can he slip under the radar when it comes to dressing in an ordinary suit, one which fits his needs perfectly in Dublin. At Downton they can hardly talk of anything else. Constant reference is made to the fact that Tom hasn't dressed for dinner – it is to them an absurdity that he owns no white tie, black tie or even morning suit for the wedding. Robert says he looks like 'a travelling salesman'; Violet calls him 'the Man from the Prudential'. Caroline McCall, the costume designer, reflected this in her suit for Tom: 'We give him more of a city look – no Donegal tweeds. Branson is a journalist living in Dublin. We wanted him to look different and out of place.' Sybil is apologetic to her family – 'we live a completely different kind of life' – but for Tom, the clothes the aristocracy wear at different events are more than simply practical or aesthetic, they are a sort of uniform for their beliefs. As such, Tom doesn't want to subscribe to them, and anyway, he has no spare money to buy extra suits for visiting his in-laws.

Branson I'm sorry, but I'm afraid I can't turn into someone else, just to please you.
Violet More's the pity.

The question of etiquette generally could serve to unhinge an outsider. While there were spoken rules, there were thousands of unspoken ones, too – things that seemed to be in place only to catch someone out. This could be distinctly unnerving. Leech felt this in more ways than one: 'Tom is very aware that he doesn't know the etiquette,' he says. 'I felt that myself, as an actor. I had never filmed those scenes in the dining room at Highclere before. I felt as if I was in the wrong place. It all seemed another world.' According to Gareth Neame, executive producer, this is reflected in the development of Branson's character in the show: 'The great thing about the second series – and beyond – is that whereas with a first series one just has a blank piece of paper and an idea about characters, by the second series those characters have been realised by actors and that very much influences our decisions. And of course one sees characters breaking through – such as Branson – who started as smaller characters but become much loved and we expand them beyond what we'd originally envisaged.'

The story of Sybil and Branson has its roots in a tale Julian heard of an earl's daughter who ran off with a groom (in that case, though, the father managed to prevent her actually marrying him). 'For the younger ones it became a family joke,' says Julian, 'but the older ones found it much harder to find him suddenly sitting there at lunch. It was a random event, as they saw it, and the point about the deferential system was that it wasn't random. So to find a chauffeur upstairs, as the Crawleys do, makes it seem as if everything might fall apart.' Coming so soon after the war, the sensation that the world will never be the same again is disturbing for the older generation, whereas the younger members of the household have less difficulty in accepting Sybil's surprising choice of husband.

Matthew I've told you before, if we're mad enough to take on the Crawley girls, we have to stick together.

Indeed, Matthew becomes something of an ally for Tom – they are to be brothers-in-law, after all. Matthew's future role as head of the family means that he is conscious that he must do what he can to make Tom feel comfortable and at home. He is also of the mind that change is not only happening now but is also a good thing. And, as Leech says, 'Matthew came to Downton as an outsider, too. He's also learning how to operate in that world. They have that bond.'

Carson Is there something we can do, sir?

Branson I just wanted to come down to say hello. I wouldn't want you to think I'd got too big for my boots.

Even the servants find it difficult to adjust to this new situation. To do their job and live the lives they lead requires that they sign up to the 'deferential system', and Tom staying above stairs and then popping downstairs throws them into confusion as much as it does their counterparts in the drawing room. It makes them positively dizzy. Carson disapproves, naturally enough, sarcastically quoting Tom: 'Mary keeps us informed.' The problem is, says Carson, Tom gives himself away with every word. 'His lordship would never call her "Mary" when he was talking to me. Never. If he wants to play their game he'd better learn their rules.'

Cora has different worries on her mind when it comes to her daughter. As she reminds Edith, 'Our blood is much less blue than the Crawleys'. Your father may be against Branson coming back to Downton, but I'm not.' Rather, she will be thinking about the chances her daughter's marriage has of surviving. Thanks to her mother, Martha Levinson, Cora will have been kept well informed of these sorts of cross-class weddings, which seemed to happen rather more often in America, attracting a great deal of press attention.

In 1910, a Miss Julia French, 'of Newport and Fifth Avenue' (very rich, in other words), eloped with her father's chauffeur, Jack Geraghty. They had a child but divorced not long after. French stated that 'It was not the fact that a man had no money which made marriage between a Society Girl and a "nobody" impractical. It was rather the difference of the point of view of the husband and wife.' Mr Geraghty had lacked that 'intangible something that springs from social background, a sense of sportsmanship and a feeling for the social values of life'. There were several other members of the '400' – the leading families of East Coast society – who made similar matches, usually ending in the divorce court. Eugenia Kelly Davis married a 'well-known Broadway dancer', Edith Webb Miles married a groom, while her elder sister ran off with a policeman. So while Cora and Martha may not have been shocked by Sybil's choice, they would have been anxious about its chances of success.

Sybil Somehow none of it seems to matter when we're in Dublin. Class and all that just seems to fade away. I'm Mrs Branson and we get on with our lives like millions of others.

Violet is perhaps the most pragmatic of everybody. She does not pretend to understand her granddaughter, but now that the thing has been done she seeks to make the best of it by dampening any gossip that will otherwise spread like wildfire through the village. 'If we show the county he can behave normally, they will soon lose interest in him,' she tells Isobel, adding as only she can: 'And I know he'll behave normally because I'll hold his hand on the radiator until he does.'

Branson I can't go through too many more dinners like last night.

Matthew You don't make it easy for them. Do you really think you can recruit Cousin Robert for Sinn Fein?

Sybil herself is in an awkward position. She loves her husband and defends his right to fight for what he believes in, which is not to say she believes in exactly the same things. Nevertheless, she is ready to immerse herself in their new life together in Dublin. She is happy to drop her title and style herself as 'Mrs Branson', living a simple existence in which they do not dress for dinner nor concern themselves with Society. She even hints that she is prepared to bring up their expected child as a Catholic, according to Tom's wishes.

'She doesn't want Tom to alter,' says Jessica Brown Findlay, who plays Sybil, 'she loves him for his fire and passion, and his desire to change things.' But when they come home she doesn't want to cause unnecessary fuss – she adores her family and respects their desire to live as they wish. Unlike Tom, she sees no harm in it. Trying to keep harmony is almost more than she can bear. Sybil confides in Mary – the sister she is closest to – that things are hard, with little money and her husband feeling patronised when they come to Downton. 'But you don't regret it?' asks Mary. 'Oh, no. Never. Not at all. He's a wonderful, wonderful man. I just wish you knew him,' says Sybil, and starts to cry.

This new lifestyle is reflected in Sybil's dresses. 'I've given her a much more bohemian look,' says McCall. 'A lot of printed fabrics, which were very modern, on sack-like, shapeless dresses. They were more practical and are also more comfortable now that she is pregnant. But for when she comes home to Downton she takes out one of her old dresses, so that she fits in with everyone else.'

For Sybil, the most pressing concern is her pregnancy and the impending birth. Childbirth at any time can make a mother-to-be feel nervous, but in the early twentieth century there were a number of what we would think of as fairly ordinary medical complications that could not, then, be easily resolved. Between 1920 and 1924, there were 76.8 stillbirths recorded for every 1,000 live births in England and Wales (now it's 3.5 per 1,000). Sybil was lucky – as the daughter of a rich man she would have anaesthetic made available to her. The poor had to make do with gripping a knotted towel. But to prepare for the birth there would have been little information available to enlighten her, other than what Cora could tell her, unless she could lay her hands on a copy of the controversial book *Family Love* by Marie Stopes, which was published in 1918 and reprinted several times in the first few weeks. A year later, Stopes wrote a sequel, *Wise Parenthood*. Besides comments on childbirth, the books detail methods of contraception, seen by her as key to female emancipation, including the use of 'a large flat sponge soaked in olive oil'. The results, needless to say, were variable. A popular rhyme at the time ran: 'Jeanie, Jeanie, full of hopes/ Read a book by Marie Stopes/ But to judge from her condition/ She must have read the wrong edition'. Stopes herself had delivered a stillborn baby after the midwife and doctor refused to let her give birth on her knees, as she had wished. She later said her baby had been 'murdered' by the arrogance and ignorance of the medical profession.

Sybil But I will not be free with our child's chances! We need peace and safety. Downton can offer us both.

At least Sybil can count on the support of her husband, whatever happens. They are a loving couple with a great deal of mutual respect. Brown Findlay says of the pair: 'There are moments of bickering. But they are very open with each other. They sort things out together. They treat each other as equals, despite their different backgrounds.' While the situation in Ireland looks to them as if it might rage for some time yet, they do at least have the refuge of Downton Abbey to keep them safe. Tom may not want to be there much, but Sybil draws comfort from her family and her childhood home; she looks to her father to give them his blessing so that they and their child may always be able to return in times of trouble, as much as she hopes for their long and happy life together.

There was a subtle language of hats: small differences conveyed much information, especially about class. Branson's soft felt 'Fedora' would have been recognised as being distinctly lower-middle class compared to the smarter, more aristocratic and stiffer-brimmed 'Homburg'.

All the Crawley girls would have played with the family dolls' house in the nursery; a scale model of the house would have been made by the estate carpenter. Unlike Queen Mary's dolls' house, which was made, in 1924, to designs by Sir Edward Lutyens, the Crawleys' is a conventional townhouse. The best producers of miniature furniture and artefacts were all German firms, but they ceased to be patronised by the British after the war.

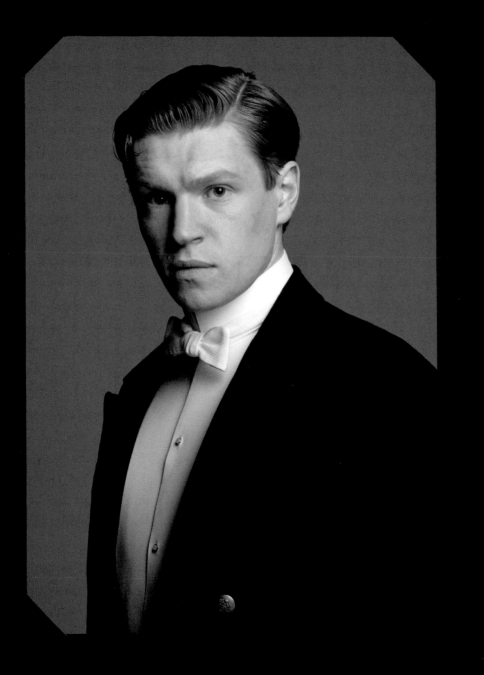

MR ALFRED NUGENT

FOOTMAN

A young footman like Alfred would quickly be brought up to speed on gentlemen's clothes and fine tailoring, as he would be expected to attend any male guests staying at Downton without their own valet. Cleaning, ironing, laying out and packing clothes all came within his remit, as did mending jobs such as sewing on buttons. Also, a footman might remove change from a gentleman's trouser pockets to make the trousers hang better – and to supplement his own wages.

R & GRANT

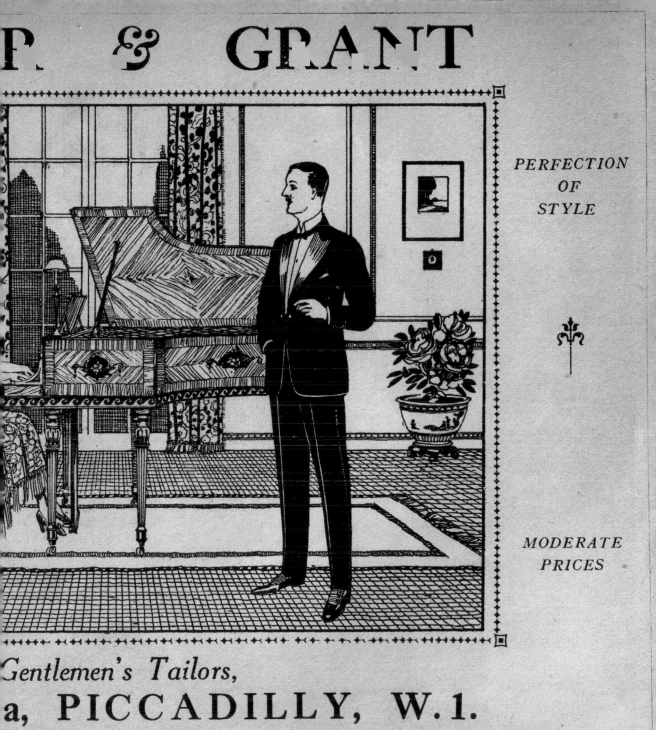

Gentlemen's Tailors,

a, PICCADILLY, W.1.

'Phone: Regent 4899.

O'Brien Pay no attention. You've got a nice manner, Alfred. You're not vain like Thomas. They'll like that.

Alfred Nugent does not have the most auspicious of starts to his new job as footman at Downton Abbey. As the nephew of Miss O'Brien, he is hardly likely to be embraced warmly into the fold, nor, despite his long search for a footman after the war, is Carson pleased by Alfred's arrival: Lady Grantham appointed him without his say-so, thanks to O'Brien's plotting. Furthermore, as Carson huffily points out, he is 'too tall. No footman should ever be over 6 foot.' And to further complicate matters, Alfred has no experience as a footman – he was a soldier in the war and then worked in a hotel. His appointment looks unlikely to ensure the smooth running of Downton Abbey.

Fortunately, Alfred is not cunning like his aunt but rather guileless and sweet. As Matt Milne, the actor playing him, says: 'He is determined to make it work. It's a big opportunity, and he is just going to keep his head down and work hard.' Even Lady Mary thinks he's nice, albeit that he looks 'like a puppy who's been rescued from a puddle'. Daisy takes a shine to him, but of course she lacks the daring to do anything about it – although the bold and modern ways of Reed, Martha Levinson's American maid, may teach her otherwise. Milne thinks Alfred laps up the attention: 'He leads Daisy on a bit – which isn't very good. I think he probably doesn't have a very good understanding of relationships from his parents. And then in the army he would have seen people having casual flings. He enjoys the affection that he receives in the servants' hall. He doesn't block Daisy and then he's blind-sided by Reed. He discovers that there is an enjoyable life to be had at Downton.'

Alfred Why are you being so nice to me?

Reed Because I like you.

Alfred And you can say it? Just like that?

Reed I'm an American, Alfred, and this is 1920. Time to live a little.

Thomas, needless to say, is jealous – Alfred has taken O'Brien's support and attention away from him. Later, as Alfred proves he means to try his best, even Carson begins to thaw. (Thomas is furious and inevitably plots trouble for the novice.) Milne explains that, for Alfred, Carson takes on even more significance: 'From my understanding, I don't think my mother is in service, or that she is that close to her sister. Also, I don't think my dad's been around much. That's one of the reasons I come to see Carson as a sort of father figure.' For such an unassuming young man, Alfred has caused quite a stir below stairs.

But then, footmen were employed to be noticed. The best footmen were good-looking and of a decent height (though no taller than the butler) and a pair of footmen were preferably of similar height, as it looked better when they were standing together. In their fine livery, often fitted by tailors in Savile Row, they looked quite splendid. After the First World War there was a great decline in the number of male indoor servants and only the grandest of families continued to keep them, making them more of a status symbol than ever – particularly as an annual tax was levied for each male servant. With Lord Grantham's money worries on his mind, the hiring of a new footman wouldn't go down well at all.

Carson would be rattled by Alfred's lack of experience; usually a footman was appointed having risen through the servant ranks. A young boy, say around 13 or 14 years old, would start as a boots or hall boy, graduating to second footman, up to first footman and then butler. Nor does Alfred appear to have much ambition for the job; in fact, as he confides to Daisy, he'd really rather be a cook, but at that time that was a career path that was harder for a man to follow than a woman. 'For every Escoffier or Monsieur Carême, you'll find a thousand dogsbodies taking orders from a cross and red-faced old woman,' he tells her (much to Mrs Patmore's displeasure).

Carson You're sure you can manage this?

Alfred Quite sure, Mr Carson.

Carson There's nothing hot. It's not a shooting lunch. Give them some champagne first, and that'll allow you time to set it out properly.

Carson Miss O'Brien, we are about to host a Society wedding. I've no time for training young hobbledehoys.

Still, being a footman was considered less taxing and far smarter than most other jobs available to a young man of his position. Nor is it remarkable for Alfred to have got his job through his aunt – servants often found work through family connections. Arthur Inch, a butler who was one of the advisors on *Gosford Park*, was the son of a butler himself, growing up on a landed estate in Yorkshire. He got his first job as a houseboy at Aldborough Hall, Boroughbridge. Before he started, his father showed him how to iron a suit correctly, to lay out a gentleman's clothes, to clean hunting clothes and to dismantle, clean and reassemble a 12-bore shotgun, in case he was required as a loader. 'I was also passed on to footmen who taught me many of their duties, such as how to mix plate-powder with ammonia and clean the tarnish off silver.' One can imagine that his first boss was delighted with his new, learned recruit.

A footman's duties brought them into quite a bit of contact with the family and its guests upstairs. They would open doors, take notes for messages, and also act as valets for any visitors who came to stay without their own servants. When travelling in their employer's car they would sit in front with the chauffeur, ready to open the door and help passengers in and out. More unobtrusively, the footmen would lay the table for breakfast, lunch and supper, take the dishes up from the kitchens and wait at table (wearing white gloves, so as not to leave fingerprints on the plates or glasses); they would also clear tables. In between meals, they attended to fires and helped to serve tea in the library or drawing room.

Their visibility meant their deportment had to be exceptional. 'Alastair [Bruce, the on-set historical advisor] is always very quick to draw attention to posture,' says Milne. 'It should be straight as a board. But there are lots of other things, little details. The position of your hands is very important. They should never be held in front of you. Ideally, in a formal situation, your thumbs should be running down the seams of your trousers.' Learning these things could be taxing, but, as Milne explains, for him it was a good thing: 'Alfred wouldn't have known about these things either. He would be learning them too. So you can feed these details into the performance.'

Alfred would rather have entered service as a cook, so he is often found lingering in the kitchen longer than most footmen.

There were some perks to this role, one of which was being able to sell the empty wine bottles and used corks that came down from the dining room – sometimes as part of an elaborate scam. One former hall boy remembered: 'These had a second-hand value and every so often a man would call to collect them, giving me twopence or threepence a dozen for the bottles. Corks could bring in much more. All the wines we served were vintage and had the year and origin stamped on the corks. An exceptional year for Champagne, claret and port could fetch as much as five shillings, and a good year, one and six to two shillings. They were resold to villains, who put them into cheap bottles with forged labels, or to wine waiters at expensive hotels and restaurants. Wine waiters were expected to put the corks of the bottles at the side of the table for the host to see; so a tipsy host paid vintage prices for cheap wines.'

With the rules changing so rapidly above stairs and below, Alfred has a harder time than most to find his feet. Luckily for him, he is a straightforward kind of chap and he will be OK if he keeps his head down and gets on with the job. Alfred is being guided by an old hand, which helps, as is Milne himself. Milne admits: 'Brian [Percival, the director] is brilliant. His notes are succinct but very useful. In one scene with Carson, he told me, "Talk to him as though he's your commanding officer. That initially was their relationship."' After the horrors of war, a life of waiting at table and flirting with the maids may have seemed very pleasant indeed. Let's hope it stays that way.

Young footmen learned about wine and how to serve it from the butler, who was responsible for the cellars. The First World War had played havoc with French wine production; many Champagne vineyards had been destroyed by the conflict. In 1919, the French Government introduced AOC (Appellation D'Origine Controlle) to regulate the quality and integrity of the different wine regions.

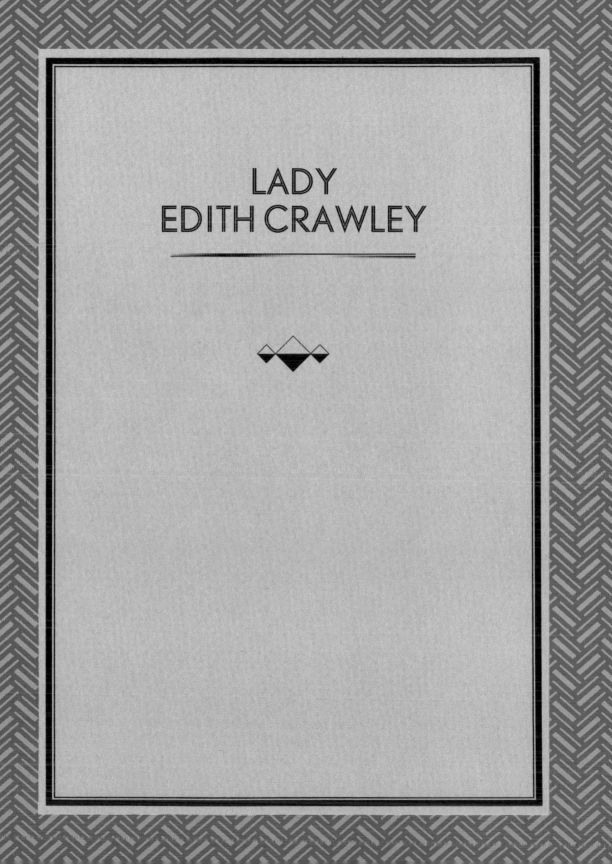

LADY
EDITH CRAWLEY

The TATLER

Vol. LXVIII. No. 884.
London, June 5, 1918

REGISTERED AT THE GENERAL
POST OFFICE AS A NEWSPAPER

Price
One Shilling

Hugh Cecil, Victoria Street

LADY RANDOLPH CHURCHILL MARRIES AGAIN

(INSET, MR. MONTAGU PHIPPEN PORCH, THE BRIDEGROOM)

Lady Randolph Churchill's engagement to Mr. Montagu Phippen Porch was announced at the end of last week, and it is understood that the marriage will take place very shortly. Before she married the late Lord Randolph Churchill in 1874 Lady Randolph was Miss Jennie Jerome of New York. She subsequently married Mr. George Cornwallis-West, whom she divorced. Mr. Montagu Porch is the son of a Bengal civil servant. He served in the Imperial Yeomanry in the South African War and has been British Resident in Northern Nigeria

Edith would have kept herself up to date with popular culture by reading *The Sketch*. Together with *The Tatler*, this was the illustrated weekly most favoured by the British upper classes in the 1920s. Its extensive coverage and numerous photographs of Society events made it the *Hello!* magazine of its day. It also included film reviews, short stories (by Agatha Christie, amongst others) and cartoons by H. E. Bateman.

The Sketch.

PRICE ONE SHILLING; BY INLAND POST, 1/2   PUBLISHING OFFICE: 172, STRAND, LONDON, W.C. 2

"Signs of Summer" Number

Cora You are being tested. And you know what they say, my darling? Being tested only makes you stronger.

Edith I don't think it's working with me.

E dith Crawley, the middle daughter of the Granthams, sandwiched between her elder, beautiful and fiery sister Mary, and Sybil, the younger, worthy one, struggles to find her position in life. She is caught between acting tough and being on the defensive. 'She's vulnerable,' says Laura Carmichael, who plays her. 'She's the disappointing daughter. And she feels that very keenly – she so wants to be loved and accepted, rather than rejected. And she throws herself into things to try and achieve that.'

For a long time, Edith believed her salvation would come in the form of a husband, but she gained no suitors as a debutante and afterwards those she liked were not available – whether Patrick Crawley, Mary's first fiancé, or John Drake, the married farmer. It was only during the war that she discovered the possibility of another kind of independence, one which allowed her to feel better about herself. She learned to drive motor cars and a tractor and proved to be invaluable to the convalescing officers, getting singled out for praise by a visiting general. Edith surprised herself, certainly, but the rest of the family were also taken aback. They, too, had been guilty of pigeon-holing Edith as a likely spinster, someone who was a bit difficult, if understandably so. The war exposed Edith's sensitive side, as Sybil tells her, 'You're far nicer than you were before the war, you know.'

But now the war is over, Edith's sisters are either engaged or married, with Sybil expecting a baby, too. The feeling of having been put back on the shelf to gather dust is creeping up on Edith, and once again she believes that only a husband will give her purpose. Her attention fixes for a second time on Sir Anthony

Strallan, now crippled by a lame arm – an injury he sustained during the war. He, at least, will need her, but more than that, Edith finds that she is genuinely fond of him. It's hard to tell if she is really in love with him but, as Carmichael says, 'He treats her like a grown-up. They can talk about books and things – and probably no one else has ever done that.'

Edith Oh please understand! I don't love you in spite of your needing to be looked after. I love you because of it.
I want you to be my life's work.

The pressure is on Edith. Not only must she defend what seems to her to be a perfectly reasonable marriage (Mary has her sordid past, Sybil has run off with the chauffeur, yet she must be denied a gentleman?), but all around her would be constant reminders that so long as she remained unmarried, she was just one amongst the ranks of the 'surplus women' in society.

It was clear to everybody after the war that women outnumbered men, but it was the 1921 Census that officially revealed that there were in fact over one and three-quarter million more women than men. That was nearly two million women who would never have the chance of romance, let alone of marriage and a family. What's more, of the men who had survived the war, 1,663,000 were wounded; many of these injured soldiers would not be capable of work, marriage or fathering children. The press was quick to whip up the panic for single women, naming them as 'surplus' – with some editorials even suggesting that these women should emigrate to Canada and the Colonies in much the same way as convicts had been shipped to Australia. Edith, painted as the spinster sister, desperately seeking marriage and with no war duties to fulfil, could be left in no doubt that she was to be pitied, useful merely as a help to her parents.

Yet, much as it would be now, this was a deeply patronising and erroneous view. Yes, there were many women who wanted their own love story, and still others who were left heartbroken after their fiancés and husbands were killed in the war, but there were also others who saw that they had been freed from the potential tyranny of marriage. Not just women who had seen their mothers and sisters bound to controlling, even cruel, husbands, but those who had had

Edith If you're going to talk about your wretched arm again, I won't listen.

Strallan It's not just my arm. I'm too old for you. You need a young chap, with his life ahead of him.

a decent education and had enjoyed their first taste of freedom and independence during the war and now wanted to make a life of it. As Miss Florence Underwood, representing the view of the Women's Freedom League, wrote to the *Daily Chronicle*: 'Marriage is not the only profession which women want … To call any woman "surplus" because she is not married is sheer impertinence.'

Before the war, many women of Edith's class suffered almost interminable boredom. Viscountess Mersey recalled: 'At Bowood during the winter I had my horse and I went hunting twice a week. On the other days I had nothing to do at all. I used to do the crossword and take my dog out, and that was about all … There was no question of doing any work. I think I did one or two things like the Young Conservatives Association, and went to meetings, and collected half-crown subscriptions, that sort of thing. I think most of my friends now would say that they were very bored.'

Edith There's nothing to do at the house except when we entertain.

Violet There must be something you could put your mind to.

Post-war, things began to change; there were exciting developments. During the war, women had shown themselves as capable, hardy and patriotic, taking on a great deal of taxing work, whether nursing, factory work or agricultural labour. Peace ended all that, as there was a strong feeling in the country that the women should stand aside and allow returning servicemen to resume their positions. Nevertheless, there was a belief that the great contribution made by Britain's females needed to be recognised and rewarded. This was one of the drivers behind the passing of the Representation of the People Act in 1918, which gave the vote to property-owning women who were over 30 years old. (Another factor was anxiety fuelled by accounts of the ongoing Russian Revolution; there was concern that a refusal to yield to demands for women's suffrage might lead to revolution at home.)

Further legislation in 1919 opened up some of the professions, including banking, accountancy, medicine and engineering, to women. The actual benefits of the new franchise were tantalisingly out of the reach of Edith and her

sisters – all of them being under 30. Nevertheless, something of the sense of possibility and self-confidence hung in the air.

The young, too, were enjoying unprecedented freedom. Before the war women lived with their parents until they married, and men enjoyed only slightly more autonomy if they attended university, leaving home to work once they were over the age of 21. Now both sexes were moving into small flats in London (although not together), driving motor cars and having fun. Surviving the war had left them with the feeling that life was short and had to be grabbed and lived. The older generations felt the sadness of their numerous bereavements hang heavily over them for years, but the young rose up with energy and daring like a phoenix from the ashes. One young woman, looking back at that time, wrote: 'Am I imagining the golden burst of intoxicating high spirits which seemed to enfold England for several years after the First World War? I don't think so … The sacrifices had been terrible, but one assumed that the result was worth it … The young men who were lucky enough to have survived felt like St Georges, who, having once and for all slaughtered the dragon, were clearly entitled to the pleasures of conquering heroes.'

Tales of the privileged few, together with some of the desperate, were soon doing the rounds – 'bottle parties' were supposedly scenes of drunken debauchery, morphine and cocaine were the drugs of choice, and dancing round the gramophone went on noisily until the small hours. London's nightclubs were flourishing – from Café de Paris to Ciro's and the Embassy – with their dimly lit, hot insides providing the perfect conditions in which heady affairs could bloom. This behaviour was not widespread and the public was shocked by reports of such shenanigans, but the young did discover a newfound confidence and an awareness that they no longer had to do what their parents told them.

Lady Manville It's exciting, Lord Grantham. I feel like one of those bright young people they write about in the newspapers.

But up in Yorkshire, Edith would have struggled to draw courage from these vibrant and independently minded young people – they were too far away, too wild, to be relevant to her situation. Stuck at home, Edith is distracted only by thoughts of enticing Strallan into marriage. Her loving father, to whom she is close, is not at all keen on the idea; Strallan is so much older and is only going to need more and more care as he ages. Robert looks at his feisty, capable daughter and cannot bear to give her up to a life of nursing. Edith doesn't see that she has much choice.

Edith How can you not like him because of his age? When almost every young man we grew up with is dead! Do you want me to spend my life alone?

Carmichael believes that Edith's natural ally is Violet – 'I think she takes her moral outlook on things from Granny' – but she also finds support from Martha, Cora's mother. It is Martha, rather than Violet, who believes Edith should be encouraged in her romantic ambitions with Strallan. Even Cora is not averse to the idea. She would rather her daughter was happily occupied than a lonely spinster, rattling around Downton Abbey. Edith's sisters aren't terribly much help in her cause – Sybil is fonder of Edith, but too preoccupied with her own worries, and while Edith's relationship with Mary is better than it was, they antagonise each other nonetheless. 'It's her insecurity and jealousy that makes her do mean things,' says Carmichael. 'She would love to be able to patronise Mary for once. And if she thinks she sees a chance, then she can't hide her nasty streak. When her own selfish needs come to the fore, she's not good at hiding it. And when Mary pushes her superiority in her face too much, she can't help reacting. Nevertheless, they definitely love each other. Edith just can't help competing.'

Before the war, Mary never lost an opportunity to put Edith down, particularly when it came to her looks. The older sister was only too pleased to flaunt her beauty, knowing that it brought her the engagement of the then heir, Patrick Crawley; even though she didn't much care for him herself, she knew that Edith was in love with him. When the mysterious 'P. Gordon' arrived at Downton claiming to be the long-lost Patrick Crawley, it looked for Edith as if she might get her chance again. Of course, as her luck would have it, he soon disappeared. But at least she is not pathetic. What with her stolen kisses from

Mr Drake and reciprocated interest from 'P' and Strallan, she knows what it is to be desired. This has given her a confidence she didn't have before, and her wardrobe in Series 3 reflects this.

'Her character had an awkwardness before, but I wanted her to have more sense of her own style in this series as she finds her feet in the world,' says the costume designer, Caroline McCall. 'Her clothes are slightly more practical, especially her daywear. Laura [Carmichael] particularly likes one of her outfits. It's very simple, just a dark-amber blouse, with three-quarter-length sleeves, a square neck, and embroidery details at the waist. It has a straight skirt in a darker tone.' Skirts of this period were generally straight, less A-line than before and more flattering. Another dress has a Grecian influence, 'a loose, fluid shape in a coral colour, with a rope belt and a beaded trim. It is shot chiffon over silk; double layers were a feature of the time, but essentially it is very simple.' As with all the women, it is the hat that is the obligatory finishing touch, and fortunately for Edith she 'looks particularly good in hats with a low crown and a wide brim'.

'Robert She'll be a nurse, Cora. And by the time she's 50, she'll be wheeling around a one-armed old man.

Whether marriage is Edith's fate or not, we cannot yet know. We do know that despite what she thinks, a husband is not her only lifeline. Edith may be an isolated character but she is not unpopular. She plays the piano well, she makes an effort with her dress, she has a sense of class and position (while she is friendly with the servants, she doesn't confide in them). Most importantly of all, she is always able to pick herself up, dust herself down, and carry on with her head held high. Of all the characters, she is the one who stands to gain the most from the new opportunities on offer. If Edith takes them, she could create real change for herself and break free of the traditions of the past to give herself a completely different kind of life from the one she has been brought up to expect. As Brian Percival, director, comments, 'Edith is a wonderful character, one of my personal favourites ... she has a complexity which has yet to be explored. Now is the right time for her to come of age and develop into a strong-willed young woman in a time of great change for women generally.' For Edith, the end of the war is just the beginning of her future.

Edith embraces the greater freedom enjoyed by women in post-war Britain. A visit to her aunt in London reveals her newfound confidence.

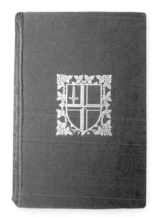

The bedside biscuit barrel was a symbol of leisured upper-class living. The biscuits – usually *petit beurre* – were supposed to stave off 'night starvation'. But, as one newspaper article suggested, they were 'a dentist's delight': 'There are few things worse for the teeth than the growing habit of nibbling a biscuit last thing at night.'

MRS PATMORE
— & —
DAISY

THE COOK &
THE KITCHEN MAID

cream or milk, butter, 1 teaspoonful of finely-chopped parsley, cayenne, salt and pepper.

METHOD.—Add the parsley and a little pepper to the ham. Coat 4 small deep patty-pans thickly with butter, over which sprinkle the ham preparation, then add an egg, breaking them carefully so as to keep the yolks whole. Season with salt, pepper, and cayenne, add a teaspoonful of cream, and place on the top a morsel of butter. Put the tins in the oven in a sauté pan, surround them to half their depth with boiling water, and poach until the white is firm. When ready, turn the eggs carefully out of the tins on to the toast, and serve.

TIME. — 15 minutes. AVERAGE COST, 1s. 2d. to 1s. 4d. SUFFICIENT for 4 persons. SEASONABLE at any time.

EGGS, POACHED, WITH SPINACH.

INGREDIENTS.—6 eggs, 1 pint of spinach purée, either fresh or tinned, 1 oz. of butter, 1 tablespoonful of brown sauce, 1 teaspoonful of lemon-juice or vinegar, nutmeg, salt, pepper, and sippets of toasted bread.

METHOD.—Prepare the spinach purée, place it in a saucepan, add the butter, a good pinch of nutmeg, salt, pepper, and the brown sauce, and make thoroughly hot. Meanwhile, poach the eggs and turn them neatly. Turn the spinach on to a hot dish, flatten the surface lightly ; upon it place the eggs and garnish with sippets of toasted bread. Serve good gravy or brown sauce separately.

TIME.—20 minutes after the purée is made. AVERAGE COST, 1s. 4d. SUFFICIENT for 5 or 6 persons. SEASONABLE at any time.

EGGS, POACHED, WITH TOMATO SAUCE.

INGREDIENTS.—6 eggs, 4 ozs. of rice, 1 oz. of butter, ¼ pint of tomato sauce, about ½ pint of stock, salt and pepper.

METHOD.—Wash and drain the rice, add it to the boiling stock, cook gently until all the stock has become absorbed, leaving the rice soft and dry, then stir

in the butter and season to ta Poach the eggs until firm and them neatly. Arrange the rice lig on a hot dish, place the eggs upor and pour the hot sauce round serve.

TIME.—1¼ hours. AVERAGE C 1s. 4d. SUFFICIENT for 5 or 6 pers SEASONABLE at any time.

EGGS, SAVOURY.

INGREDIENTS.—4 eggs, 4 round buttered toast, 2 ozs. of finely-chop cooked ham, 1 teaspoonful of fin chopped parsley, salt and peppe

METHOD.—Butter 4 small ch ramakin cases or dariol moulds, coat them thickly with ham and p ley, previously mixed together. B an egg carefully into each case, sprinkle them with salt and pep Bake or steam until firm, then them on to the prepared toast, serve.

TIME.—10 to 15 minutes. AVER COST, 10d. SUFFICIENT for 3 (persons. SEASONABLE at any tim

EGGS, SCOTCH.

INGREDIENTS.—3 hard-boiled e ½ lb. of sausages, 1 raw egg, br crumbs, frying-fat, fried parsley croûtes of fried bread.

METHOD.—Skin the sausages, them together and divide into 3 e parts. Shell the eggs, enclose ther the sausage-meat, coat with egg breadcrumbs, and fry in hot fat, w should be sufficiently deep to c them. Drain well, cut them in hal dish them on the croûtes, and s garnished with parsley. Tomato s frequently accompanies this dish.

TIME.—½ an hour. AVERAGE C 1s. to 1s. 3d. SUFFICIENT for 3 persons. SEASONABLE at any tim

EGGS, SCRAMBLED.

INGREDIENTS.—4 eggs, 2 slice buttered toast, 1 oz. of butter, 2 ta spoonfuls of cream or milk, salt pepper, chopped parsley.

METHOD.—If liked, round, ova triangular croûtes of toasted bread be used, but for ordinary purposes slice of toast may be trimmed and

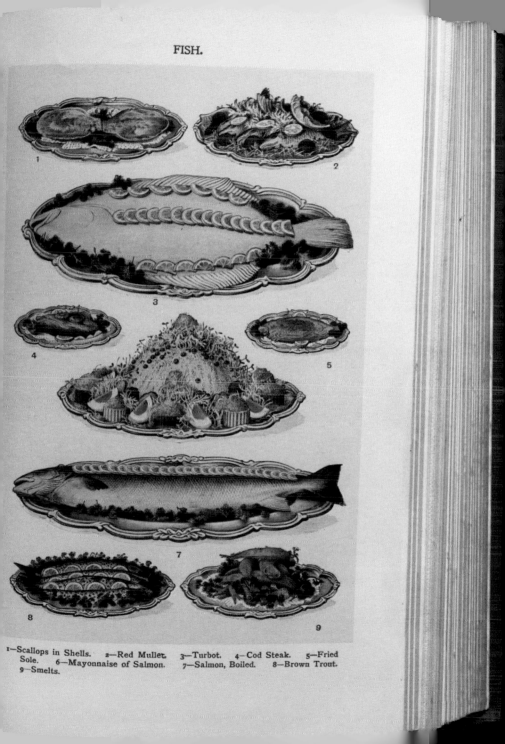

1—Scallops in Shells.   2—Red Mullet.   3—Turbot.   4—Cod Steak.   5—Fried Sole.   6—Mayonnaise of Salmon.   7—Salmon, Boiled.   8—Brown Trout. 9—Smelts.

Mrs Patmore Go to bed when you're done.

Daisy I'll go to bed when I'm ready.

Mrs Patmore What's happened to you? Have you swapped places with your evil twin?

Daisy I'd like to know where the new kitchen maid is, that's what you promised.

Changes are occurring below stairs at Downton as the drums of war cease to beat. Gareth Neame, executive producer, wants to show that new opportunities are arising for Daisy and her like, too: 'Right from the first series we have tried to show that while the family are part of the Downton establishment, many of the servants, particularly the younger ones, are searching for love or advancement or are merely passing through. From a dramatic point of view, not only might the characters show ambition and seek promotion, but in fact we also like to make use of their changed roles to vary the stories from what's happened before.' As the meek protégée of the cook, Daisy, fuelled by a desire to improve her situation, has started to find her voice and is defiantly answering back to make sure she gets what she believes is her due.

Daisy is treated as an inconsequential junior by the other servants. 'She would have had a tough childhood', says Julian Fellowes, 'so low in class that there is a greater distance between her and Carson than there is between him and Lord Grantham. They're from the functioning upper end of the scale and she's from the dysfunctional lower end.' In fact, she would have been almost rescued by Mrs Patmore. 'We know she has hardly any family at all and Mrs Patmore may have taken pity on her and brought her into the house,' says Julian. But it's the tendency of the rest to ignore her, almost hardly see her when she is in the room, that has meant Daisy has ended up being privy to some of the darker secrets of the house, tormenting her superstitious nature.

In the future, Daisy hopes to be working more closely with Mrs Patmore, taking on a greater proportion of the cooking and leaving behind the drudgery

of the last few years. This is reflected in her dress, as the costume designer, Caroline McCall, explains: 'Daisy is trying to be more grown up. We have got her into a more serious dress, moving out of pale fabrics into darker colours.' But her efforts may be in vain. 'You probably don't notice it,' reveals Sophie McShera, the actress who plays her, 'but Daisy is never allowed to sit down. She is always standing. It gets very tiring. Sometimes a new third assistant director will say, "You sit down over there," and I think, "Yes!", but I know it won't last.' While a few country-house cooks had been trained in the kitchens of international hotels – Mrs McKay, the cook at the Dashwoods' house, West Wycombe Park, had trained at The Ritz – most rose through the ranks. Daisy is on a path that can go onwards and upwards, should she not leave to marry.

She is, of course, technically called Mrs Mason, having married William on his deathbed, but she sees that as a fraud – she didn't love him and is ashamed that he loved her. Poor Daisy, so innocent and naive in her view of humanity. She's a romantic, prone to crushes: Thomas (futile, for obvious reasons) and now the new footman, Alfred Nugent. We can see that it's hard for her to conjure up the courage to do anything about it. But a trip to the picture house in York on her day off would have encouraged Daisy, had she seen *True Heart Susie*, a 1919 film starring the famous Hollywood actress Lillian Gish with Robert Harron. In this popular film Gish plays the self-effacing girl next door, in love with the dashing Harron. He goes off to college and subsequently marries a sophisticated young woman, who then dies, and Gish finally gets her man.

Such heady notions do not bother Daisy's boss, Mrs Patmore. Having worked at Downton for many years, little fazes her. The Boer War and the First World War have taken men she knew and there has been, doubtless, a succession of kitchen maids. The cook has learned to confine her worries to the kitchen, only getting hot under the collar when a soufflé fails to rise or the footman takes the wrong sauce to the dining room. The outside world and its changes only rarely affect her. 'Mrs Patmore is a product of her time,' says Lesley Nicol, the actress who plays her, 'loyal to the family, and to the household. She is very proud of her job and good at it, too, I think.'

This is not to say that she – nor any of the servants – is able to live on the estate completely shielded from the world beyond it. The war, particularly, made a great mark on their lives, with Mrs Patmore suffering considerable grief over the death of her nephew, Archie. Having left their families behind many years ago and only seeing them perhaps once or twice a year, if that, one can imagine that they would be affected by thoughts of their childhood. Nostalgia

Daisy The chimney isn't drawing properly. This oven's not hot enough.

Mrs Patmore A bad workman blames his tools.

is a powerful emotion, and perhaps explains why the older servants appear to prefer the lifestyle of the past and the old way of doing things.

The younger servants tend to be more susceptible to the changing world and its influence, partly thanks to their better education. Even Daisy, a young country girl from the lowest end of the working classes, received a fairly decent schooling. From the 1870s and 1880s onwards, there were big strides towards teaching all children literacy and numeracy. Daisy would have benefited from free compulsory schooling up to the age of ten, at least, in a way that her mother almost certainly wouldn't have: she can read and write and do simple sums. Just reading one of the tabloid newspapers would have encouraged Daisy to think differently and be more ambitious for herself.

Daisy I'm running at full strength and I always have been with no one to help me, neither.

Mrs Patmore All in good time, Daisy. All in good time.

As sole keeper of her kingdom and in charge of her own servants, Mrs Patmore has limited relationships with the others below stairs – the kitchen staff even eat separately. She is ready to help Mrs Hughes when asked, on a personal note anyway, and she respects Carson as a butler who does his job well (even if she does think he takes it a bit seriously). But otherwise Mrs Patmore keeps to herself and her staff, avoiding too much contact with the other servants, and in particular O'Brien and Thomas, of whom she has a healthy, cynical view. 'She has a strong personality, she can be quite sarcastic,' says Nicol. 'But she enjoys her wit and uses it to good effect. She reminds me of the women I grew up amongst in the North West. They were honest and direct and very funny.'

As for the family above stairs, Mrs Patmore is amusingly timid in the presence of Lord Grantham – he is the only person by whom she seems rather overawed. Lady Grantham is less of a challenge, as they talk daily to discuss the menus. But even then, Cora would be careful not to come down to the kitchens unexpectedly. And if the cook was expected to prepare lunches and dinners on schedule, the family was expected to eat them on time as well. Eileen Balderson,

who worked as a kitchen maid in a succession of country houses between the wars, recalled that if the family were late for a meal now and then nothing was said, but if it happened repeatedly, 'the mistress would soon be told about it'.

Daisy, being youthful and curious, has a more lively set of relationships within the household. Partly because her job takes her all over the house – from laying fires in the bedrooms upstairs before anyone wakes, to her kitchen duties – she has been privy to details that others miss. Not just the sleeping habits of the household (she might have been shocked at first to discover that the Earl and his wife shared a bed every night), but real secrets, as when she saw Lady Grantham, Lady Mary and Anna dragging Kemal Pamuk's corpse back to his bed. 'She's the first person to wake up in that great big house,' says Sophie McShera. 'I always think of that. How strange it must have been.'

It's understandable that she would want to move on to greater things. The lot of a kitchen maid – the lowest of all the servants – was onerous. Aside from performing a few tiresome tasks around the rest of the house, they rarely left the kitchen, even eating in there rather than in the servants' hall. The round of food preparation and pan scrubbing was ceaseless, and while potato peeling may have been tedious, other tasks were far less pleasant. Sculleries were not a place for the squeamish. Millie Milgate, who worked as a kitchen maid in the early 1920s, was alarmed to find herself being asked to 'dress a chicken'. When she admitted that she didn't know how to, the cook slapped her face and pushed her into the scullery. 'There, I was initiated in the art of bird dressing. It was greasy and smelly and I felt sick but, after several painful pokes on my arm, I was forced to go on, with the cook saying, "That's nothing my girl, wait 'til you have to do game birds that's been hanging for a month." … A few days later a hare was slung at me, which I was shown this time how to skin and gut, but I vowed never again.' (Millie resigned soon after and became a housemaid.)

Despite the new wave of labour-saving devices that Mrs Hughes is enjoying, the mechanics of a kitchen remained basic. Soft soap remained the principal cleaning agent for the majority of tasks, except for copper pans, which had to be cleaned with a mixture of salt, vinegar, sand and flour. Mixed together and rubbed on by hand, this brought the metal up to a lustrous shine, but at a price. Every kitchen maid complained bitterly of her cracked and chapped hands, which in turn made other tasks more difficult and painful. The worst of these was preparing the daily supply of cooking salt, which was done by rubbing a large block of solid salt through a sieve. 'Everything was so much more brutal then,' says McShera. 'Harder, heavier and took longer. The first time I picked

Even though they are busy running their own domains, Carson, Mrs Hughes and Mrs Patmore all support one another during difficult times.

up my [cleaning] box, it was so heavy it left big red marks on my hand. And on top of all that, everyone's shouting at you all the time.'

In an age of hospitality and show, the quality of the food a family presented to its guests was a key element in its standing and reputation. It was the cook's responsibility to deliver. Moreover, it was a task that had to be faced against the clock – six times a day, plus elevenses and tea – in an often crowded kitchen in stifling heat produced by the huge coal-fired range that was kept lit all day. That high-quality food was produced under such conditions was truly wondrous.

Some commodities remained scarce after the war. Butter and sugar were still rationed and generally supplies grew more expensive. On estimate, food prices rose by 155 per cent between 1914 and 1920. An estate such as Downton, with home farms, dairy herds and walled vegetable gardens within its grounds, would be largely unaffected by such troubles. Mrs Patmore's specialities of truffled egg on toast, oysters *à la Russe*, lobster rissoles in mousseline sauce and asparagus salad with champagne-saffron vinaigrette ensured that the dining room fare remained impressive despite the reduced availability of certain ingredients.

The sophisticated French dishes that were popular would, however, have made both Mrs Patmore and Daisy uncomfortably aware of their limited education. Much of the vocabulary of a country-house kitchen at that time was in French – the names of the dishes, the styles of preparation and the cooking methods. The young Margaret Thomas recalled how, for news of what she was supposed to be cooking and preparing each day, she was told she must 'read the slate'. This had been 'passed' by the lady of the house after her morning consultation with the cook and was always written in French: 'So I spent most of my afternoons, until I got a working knowledge of the language, studying the cookery book, which gave the names of each dish in English as well as French.'

With the long hours, the constant pressure and the uncomfortable working conditions (particularly in a hot summer), it seems quite extraordinary from our modern perspective that the servants stayed in their jobs for as long as they did. While housemaids and many of the kitchen maids tended to leave after just a few years to marry, the likes of Mrs Patmore (unmarried, the prefix is merely to give her respectable status) and Daisy, if she chooses to train as a cook, will remain in a kitchen for most of their lives. But perhaps the exit route is not easy for the kitchen staff to see, even if they think to look for it. We don't know what will happen to Daisy, whether love or ambition will come through for her and decide her fate. As for Mrs Patmore, she will stay at Downton until old age forces her to leave. 'The house was their whole world,' says Nicol.

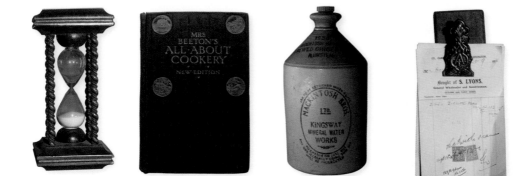

With four meals a day to be prepared for both the family and the servants, meticulous planning was essential; so, too, was good communication. Mrs Patmore, much to her annoyance, has to order all her supplies through Mrs Hughes, the housekeeper.

Although books such as *Mrs Beeton's Household Management* were a fixture in all country-house kitchens, successful cooks also kept detailed notes of their favourite recipes to serve as references for themselves and their kitchen maids. Daisy studies Mrs Patmore's recipes with the aim of bettering her position. She was just one of many working-class girls who took courage from the tenor of the times: as another young kitchen maid recalled, 'Everything was going well for women when Nancy Astor was elected.'

MATTHEW CRAWLEY ESQ.

HEIR TO THE EARLDOM
AND THE DOWNTON ESTATE

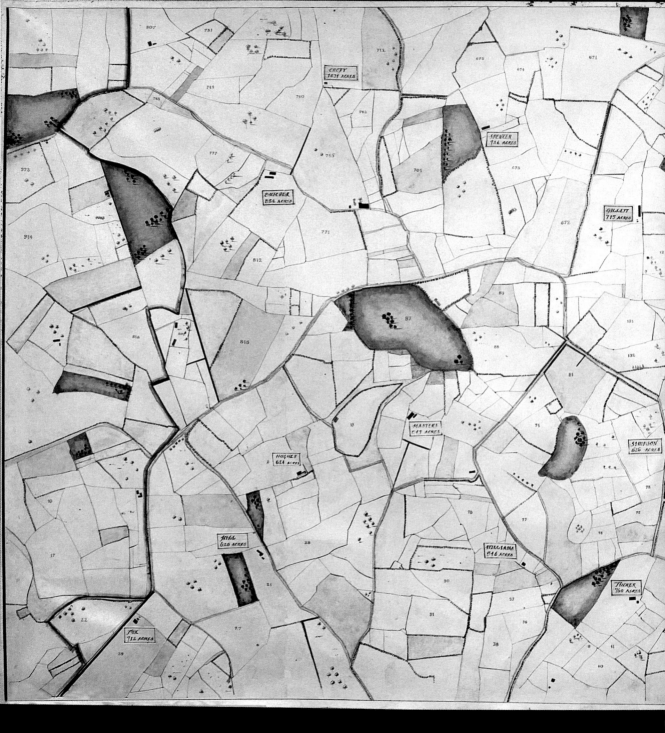

Agricultural revenues had been falling for 50 years by 1920. Although grain prices
had been artificially increased during the war, this was set to change with the coming

COLLINS
762 ACRES

EDWARDS
683 ACRES

DOWNTON ABBEY
YORKSHIRE
·MIDDLE·
SCALE
25.344 INCHES TO ONE STATUTE MILE 1 : 2500

Matthew I want us to get to know each other, to learn about who we both are without everyone being there.

Mary It is quite a big house.

Matthew It's a lovely house. It's your home and I want it to be my home, too.

M atthew Crawley is a man trying to walk in a straight line on shifting sands. Brought up as the middle-class son of a Manchester doctor, he trained to be a solicitor and was prepared for a conventional life. He expected little more than to work, marry a girl-next-door and raise a family of his own. Instead he has been thrust into the role of earl-in-waiting, in line to inherit a vast house and estate, and he has fallen in love with a woman who is not so much next-door as next-county. A fundamentally decent person, driven by a strong sense of fairness and the need to toe the moral line, in his changed circumstances Matthew finds it increasingly difficult to say with any certainty what is the right thing for him to do. It's less a question of what is right and what is wrong, so much as which 'right' he must choose: whether he upholds his principles as a modern man or those of the ancient aristocracy.

Matthew's unexpected claim to the earldom of Downton Abbey opens a door into another world, and introduces him to Mary. Thus began the love story that would encounter many obstacles before a happy end could be reached. After breaking off his first engagement to Mary because he couldn't trust her motives for marrying him, Matthew thought he had made a better decision in asking for the hand of Lavinia Swire, a sweet girl with his interests very much at heart. Only, she then died – as he believed, of a broken heart – shortly after she discovered him kissing Mary. For this, he can never forgive himself, explains Dan Stevens, who plays Matthew: 'The situation with Lavinia haunts him. He feels responsible for her death, even though that doesn't really make sense. And it takes him a long time to come to terms with that.' Indeed,

burdened by these guilty feelings, Matthew needs the passing of time and the persuasiveness of his mother to reunite him with Mary, despite his love for her. But having made the leap at last, he is determined to do his best by them both.

Matthew Are you looking forward to the wedding?
Mary What do you think?
Matthew I'm looking forward to all sorts of things.
Mary Don't make me blush.

Somehow it's rather lovely to hear Matthew enjoy the frivolous, flirtatious pleasures of a love affair. He is so frequently tortured by his conscience that one doesn't always think of him as a happy-go-lucky young man. Matthew needs to learn to enjoy their carefree moments together; their union means he is firmly part of the Grantham clan, which also means he is expected to behave in a certain fashion – in ways that are not only unfamiliar to him but that make him feel uncomfortable, too.

Matthew is the perfect symbol of the tension between the old and new worlds that was simmering away as the decade began. By the start of Series 3, he has acclimatised himself to Downton Abbey and its way of doing things, but he also sees the opportunity for change. This desire for change is not only driven by social politics, but more soberingly comes from the aftermath of the war. Matthew is the only person at Downton Abbey to have seen active service in the war and survived physically unscathed (Thomas's injury sent him home and William died of his wounds). This is a huge burden that Matthew bears, and bears alone. He, like almost all his comrades, is unwilling or unable to discuss his experiences with the civilian population. The returning soldiers were simply viewed as 'heroes' and were expected to deport themselves as such. That was enough. Everybody else was anxious to move on and away from the horrors of the war.

It was hard to escape from the searing experiences of four years of trench warfare, though. Having fought and lived, Matthew was vulnerable to those

complex feelings of remorse and regret that we now call 'survivor's guilt'. And there was, too, for all who had endured the horrors of the Front, the constant threat of nightmare images and memories which recurred unexpectedly, interrupting the flow of everyday life. The poet Robert Graves recorded how he would awake screaming from dreams of exploding German shells, and that he found strangers might suddenly assume the faces of his fallen friends, or the ringing of a telephone could induce a feeling of panic.

Now, all these reactions are recognised and treated as 'post-traumatic stress disorder', but in 1920 they were just a grim and little understood fact of existence for those who had survived the war, one shared by millions of men who were trying to readjust to life at home. And even if Matthew was not subject to the most debilitating forms of attack, he had to live with the knowledge – and the anxiety – that such feelings lurked below the surface.

But having survived the war – no mean feat when officers had a life expectancy of around six weeks on the frontline – and recovered from what had appeared to be a permanent paralysis of the lower spine, Matthew is a lucky man. What's more, he has the possibility of gaining a large fortune, and is due to marry the woman he loves.

Yet, he is not a man at ease. His conscience is easily pricked by the requirements that lie ahead of him in the role of Earl of Grantham: he was brought up to believe in social justice and he is still adjusting to the necessity of having servants do everything for him. He yearns for a simpler life but is reminded that the duty of an aristocrat is to provide employment, and though he sees that he can be a good landlord for the farming tenants, he would still rather hire men to work the land than a valet to fasten his cufflinks. But if he sacked the servants because of his personal discomfort in being a master, then he would be putting people out of work.

When it comes to the future of Downton Abbey itself, under threat now that Robert's investments have gone seriously awry, Matthew puts his principles ahead of its rescue, something that Mary finds hard to comprehend. To Matthew's surprise, Lavinia's father, Reginald Swire, has named him as an heir, but Matthew cannot see how he could ever accept the money that comes with the inheritance, because of the guilt that he feels over the way his relationship with Lavinia ended. Mary, equally fervently, feels the opposite. It is anathema to her (and her class) that he should put his feelings before his loyalty to the Crawley family and saving their ancestral seat.

Matthew I sometimes think it's time
we lived in a simpler way.

Matthew Reggie Swire will have put me in his will because he believed I was his daughter's one true love.

Mary So you were.

Matthew Yes, but I broke Lavinia's heart and she died. He never knew that. How could I possibly allow myself to profit from her death?

However, in the face of a precarious future, we know that Matthew is better equipped than Mary to anticipate and cope with the changes that will inevitably come. As the British aristocracy emerged, battered and be-taxed, into the post-war world, it became increasingly clear that alternative strategies to 'living off the land' had to be found if they were to sustain their traditional position. Marrying money was still a popular option, but increasingly the upper classes considered earning money themselves, looking to the worlds of business, finance, colonial administrations and even the professions. Lord Montagu of Beaulieu recalled: 'Individuals, prompted by the changing times, began to make their ways in fields unknown to their predecessors. Peers, often under plebeian pseudonyms, were to be found on the stage, in the cinema world, in journalism, motoring and exploration.'

In this respect, Matthew is well placed, despite the fact that he is essentially moving in the other direction. Having grounded himself in the professions, as a solicitor, he is now taking on the responsibilities of a landed aristocrat with the skills, the outlook and the earning capability of a career at his command. Strangely, despite the strong connection between the law and the aristocracy (many eldest sons of peers studied law in the nineteenth century as good preparation for running their estates and for assuming political roles), by Matthew's time, pursuing a career as a lawyer was considered rather outside the usual run. Specialisation and regulation within the profession had discouraged many of the old landed amateurs and the law had come to be seen as thoroughly

middle class. This might have been a hindrance before, but as Matthew leads Downton Abbey further into the modern era, it now appears that it will in fact be a help.

Furthermore, having experienced and survived the war, Matthew has a greater understanding of the social evolution that is now taking place. Many of the soldiers who fought in the trenches lost respect for the distant generals who commanded them with such spectacular incompetence. And while they admired and respected the young upper-class officers who led them into battle and shared their life in the trenches, this very proximity reduced their mystique. Many of the old habits of deference were lost during the years of conflict, and this affected all strata of society. Where Robert might instinctively look to George V for guidance, Matthew was unlikely to do the same. Indeed it is doubtful how much he looks to Robert, much though he loves him. He recognises that Robert's priorities are with preserving things as they are, rather than trying to change them for the better.

In other ways, though, the two are close. Matthew's father died when he was quite young, and Robert has never had a son, so the two relish the chance to build their relationship along such familial lines. There was some restraint initially on Matthew's part, as he found his footing in the aristocratic world and questioned Robert's views, but he knows that his father-in-law-to-be is a good and kind man, and that is what matters most to him. In taking on the estate, Matthew determines to be just as fair a landlord as Robert, but perhaps a more efficient and engaged one, even though this was considered unusual at the time.

Lady Hyde Parker's husband at Melford farmed his own land and drew a lot of comment for it: 'They spoke about it a great deal in the neigbourhood: "Have you heard? Willy farms, he's started farming."' It could be a shock when members of the landed classes got involved and discovered that huge amounts of money had been squandered. When Sir John and Lady Dashwood took on West Wycombe Park after the First World War, it was rundown after years of neglect. They determined to make a go of it and cut out any waste by examining how the estate had been run thus far, but they soon found that there were serious problems that had developed in the absence of any real management: 'I said we must get the family finances on a solid basis and find out what is going on, stop all this waste: six gardeners and nothing grown but cabbages; an enormous amount of acres and no money. We went into all the figures and found such cheating. The extraordinary thing was that the agent and solicitor told Johnnie that the most he could take out of the estate was £1,200 a year. I never knew if it

was true or not; I didn't know anything about the money, nor care, but when we went through the figures we found the agent was getting £2,800 and the solicitor £3,200. That didn't seem to me quite right!'

Mary Are you all right? You seem to have been slaving away for hours.

Matthew I want to be up to date with it all before I go back into the office.

Dan Stevens sees the value in Matthew being given more responsibility at Downton Abbey before he formally inherits it: 'Because of his legal background, Robert values him as someone who can bring a fresh approach to things. Also, he belongs to the younger generation and looks at things in a new way.' But, of course, Matthew is worried. 'He's slightly anxious about it. He doesn't want to feel that he's treading on Robert's toes, or to wrest the estate away from him,' says Stevens. However, as with Mary, once the decision has been made, Matthew gets behind it wholeheartedly. 'Once he does engage – after Robert reassures him – he does it very efficiently. He has to make this tough call, and he does it. He's not ruthless, but he is clear-sighted,' says Stevens.

It was a hard time. While the kindest landlords may have been reluctant to put up their tenants' rents, agricultural wages were often cut: between 1920 and 1922 in Norfolk, they fell from 46 shillings a week to 25 shillings. And while the likes of Mrs Hughes might have been starting to enjoy labour-saving devices to help her with her housekeeping, farming was still largely done using traditional methods. One landowner's wife, Mrs Charles Brocklebank, recalled: 'There was hardly any mechanisation then: we had wind pumps on the farms. I remember hearing the first tractor in the 1920s. At harvest you just heard the boy warning the man on the top of the wagon that the horse was about to move forward. That was all. You could hear him calling "Hold ye up" from far across the Cambridgeshire fields.'

Matthew may yet have the occupation of Gentleman Farmer in his future, but for the moment he's still a solicitor, and dressed as such. For the third series the costume department have introduced some country clothing for him, too: 'In his tweeds he's a younger version of Hugh [Bonneville],' says Caroline McCall,

In Matthew, Robert has found a natural successor to his earldom. His views may differ in some respects, but fundamentally he wants the same thing as his father-in-law: a future for Downton Abbey.

costume designer. 'It was an age when fine tailoring was very important. We've had a number of suits made for him.' Most important of all was the black tie – the outfit in which Matthew gets to look his most dashing to our modern eyes: 'It was acceptable then if it was just the family at dinner,' explains McCall. 'I really wanted to get the shape right for that date. Narrowing the waist of the jacket and having single-pleat trousers to give him a long shape.' The Prince of Wales (later King Edward VIII for a brief period, before he abdicated the throne to marry American divorcee Mrs Wallis Simpson) was the arbiter of fashion then and young men would follow his style. This meant softer collars during the day, worn with thick silk ties.

Matthew's challenges are not yet over. While excited at the prospect of married life, he and Mary are aware that it will not be plain sailing. Brian Percival, director, believes this relationship will continue to fascinate us, even once they are married: 'There will always remain an element of doubt as to whether their relationship will succeed. Mary in particular has her own very strong and well-defined character; she can be devious and scheming when she needs to be, and ultimately do what is best for her, often defined by wealth and power. Matthew is quite a counterpoint to this, usually putting his own moral standpoint before all else, including fortune and title. The fact that in many ways the two are chalk and cheese keeps us interested because of what this may throw up. In many ways both their lives would be much easier if they didn't have a relationship together, however the one thing they both have little control over is the fact that they have fallen in love. This is what keeps us engaged: their inner battles between what they normally believe in and how much of it either can retain in the face of their feelings for each other.'

Matthew and Mary have yet to decide where they will live as husband and wife, which is really a question of *how* they will live. She, of course, wants to stay at her home, Downton Abbey, where she hopes they will live until they die. But Matthew would like them to be independent, to begin their life together away from the gaze of the family and its servants. He wants to live in a plainer manner, one that takes less account of formalities and traditional hierarchies. He sees that the future is bright but is wise enough to acknowledge its uncertainties, and so he has no clear answers. Julian Fellowes, naturally, says it best: 'Matthew sees no point in replicating that life even if he has got comfortable with living in the house and on the estate. But that internal tension existed. Matthew represents the feeling that if it's going to survive, it's got to change – and he was right.'

Matthew's decision to buy a Humber Roadster was typical of the period. Motoring had always been considered a smart, even aristocratic, pastime. C. S. Rolls (the co-founder of Rolls-Royce) was the younger son of Lord Llangattock, while the popular journal *Car Illustrated* was owned and edited by Lord Montagu of Beaulieu.

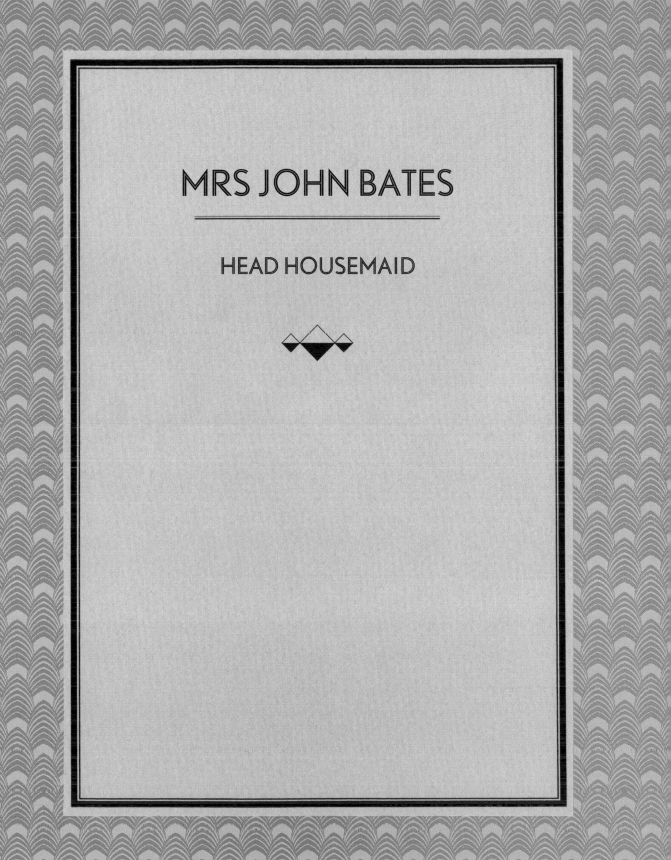

MRS JOHN BATES

HEAD HOUSEMAID

Mrs Bates
Downton Abbey
Downton

Yorkshire

Prison inmates were restricted as to the number of letters that they could send and receive. At the start of their sentence they might only be allowed to send a letter every couple of months, but with good behaviour and time, a prisoner such as Bates would pass through the so-called 'Progressive Stages' and would see his privileges steadily increase.

June 1920

My dearest Anna,

If I have loved any one as much as you it is a lie. If I have done anything my sweet that it was never intended.

Surely as I look upon this Book st Before me It contains information that will Be the key to your freedom.

Six weeks have passed since our last corresponda-nce, how I wish to know why.

Forever your Beloved,

John

Bates Do you never doubt? For just one minute? I wouldn't blame you.

Anna No. And I don't doubt that the sun will rise in the east, either.

Anna Bates is a rare creature; utterly sure of herself, dependable, sympathetic and steadfastly loyal. She is generous and kind but she's no pushover, and her steely determination to do the right thing by those she loves has earned her respect from everybody at Downton Abbey. Even hard-hearted O'Brien grudgingly accepts that Anna is good at her job and does not cross her. Only Thomas will occasionally send a barbed remark in her direction, but it's usually about Bates, not Anna herself, and she is able to give as good as she gets when it comes to defending her husband.

Of course, he takes some defending. A convicted murderer for a husband is not quite every newlywed's dream, but Anna is unwavering in her belief that he is innocent. Anna puts her loyalty to her husband first and foremost, and her love for him could be as dangerous as it is steadfast. If he is proved to be guilty after all, Anna will have been blind; but if he really is innocent, then she has been wise. Either way, she has to close herself off to the influence of others. But this she does anyway.

With Bates in York Prison, it is up to Anna to make the best of things and to handle his affairs for him as his wife. She travels to London with Mrs Hughes to get his mother's old house ready to rent out, as it's in her name now, demonstrating her practicality and ability to get on with life, whatever it throws at her. Still relatively young, Anna is 'emotionally wise for her age', says Joanne Froggatt, the actress who plays the part. 'I think she must have gone through things in her childhood. Perhaps the loss of a younger sibling. She has learnt a lot in a short time. She must have lived a life which taught her to deal with hard

times in the way that she does.' As self-reliant as Anna may be, rarely seeking help, she is quick to be there for others. In fact, she is able to empathise with almost anybody, no matter what their circumstances or what is worrying them.

With a respectable position but less seniority than Mrs Hughes, Anna is able to move fluidly between the floors of the house, more so than anybody else. She has genuine relationships across the spectrum – from the junior maids below stairs to the attachment to Lady Mary above. Molesley, the butler/valet for Mrs Crawley and Matthew, doesn't have much time for most people but he has a soft spot for Anna. (Poor Molesley. Bates gets in the way of both his heart's desire *and* his perfect job.) Even Lord Grantham is fond of Anna, as the loved one of his long-suffering valet and friend. He feels deeply sorry for her, too – despite his best efforts, Bates is sitting out a sentence that could last up to 20 years.

Bates Haven't you anything better to do?
Anna I have not. Because I'd rather
work to get you free than dine with
the King at Buckingham Palace.

But Anna has a backbone of steel and does not entertain for one moment the notion that she might not be able to uncover something that the detective on the case missed, to prove her husband's innocence. In the second half of 1920, the newspapers were full of a story that would have been preying on Anna's mind – as well as on those of others at Downton – the trial of Harold Greenwood. It had chilling echoes of the case against Bates.

Greenwood, a solicitor from Kidwelly in Wales, was accused of murdering his wife, Mabel, with arsenic, so that he could marry a much younger woman. Mabel Greenwood had died in June 1919, apparently of heart failure, and it was only after a persistent local whispering campaign had built up against Mr Greenwood and his new wife that the police decided to exhume her body and hold an inquest. They found traces of arsenic in Mabel's blood, and returned a verdict of murder by poisoning, 'administered by Harold Greenwood'. At the subsequent trial it was alleged that he had poisoned her during Sunday lunch, by means of a bottle of Burgundy.

Greenwood was fortunate to have Sir Edward Marshall Hall, a brilliant advocate of the time, as his lawyer (Bates would have fared much better if he had engaged his services). Marshall Hall undermined the forensic evidence, discredited the testimony of the parlour maid, and showed that Greenwood and Mabel's grown-up daughter had also drunk from the same bottle of wine but with no ill effects. The jury, rather reluctantly, returned a verdict of 'not guilty'. But the ill feeling against Greenwood persisted in the local area and, together with his new wife, he left Wales to start a new life under a new name. The whole case would have been a powerful reminder to Anna of the difficulties involved in both proving a man's innocence and upholding his good reputation.

Bates I don't see what can come of it.

Anna Probably nothing. And my next idea will probably lead to nothing. And the next and the next. But one day, something will occur to us, and we'll follow it up and the case against you will crumble.

In her quest to unlock the mystery she might have drawn comfort from a small volume published that same year. *The Mysterious Affair at Styles* was Agatha Christie's first novel and introduced the detective Hercule Poirot. It would have suggested, if nothing else, that in many cases things are not as they first appear. Intelligence and persistence are required to uncover the true course of events and both of these are qualities Anna possesses.

But while Anna is relentless in her sleuthing, she cannot do it all of the time, and with prison visits so limited she may be grateful for the distraction that her work brings, if nothing else. As head housemaid, Anna is eligible for a certain amount of lady's maid duties for the daughters of the house as well as any female guest who arrives to stay without her own personal servant. (The head housemaid would look after the married women, the junior maids after the unmarried guests.) Hence, Anna has got to know Lady Edith and Lady Sybil well, being privy to their chatter when getting ready for dinner or during the 20 minutes of brushing their hair before bed. Dressing hair would have been an important element of this work and as Loelia, Duchess of Westminster,

In her quest to prove her husband's innocence, Anna visits acquaintances from the first Mrs Bates's past.

recalled, it was 'not easy. It was first tied in bunches with little bits of tape and then pinned up in puffs and mounds and curls attached to long wires fixed on the side.' Curiously, at the time women believed that hair would split and 'bleed' when cut, so they would singe the ends with a lit taper after the scissors had done their work.

Lady Mary, of course, is close to Anna, perhaps more so than to anyone else, other than her fiancé, Matthew. They may have more of a shared history than we realise. 'Julian told me that it is possible that they would have played together as children,' says Froggatt. 'Or at least encountered each other. Anna probably grew up on the estate or nearby.' It's rather telling, then, that Anna never mentions her family. If they are local, why did no one come to her wedding? She never talks about them, yet one wouldn't imagine her to be the sort of person to abandon her family. Either they left her to live elsewhere or they all died in some sort of horrible epidemic, which seems rather brutal, or she is someone who keeps herself entirely to herself. This latter seems to me the most likely. For all her kindness – which is true – something has made her close herself off from most of the world. Both she and Bates share this emotional reserve, however sweet and open they are with each other.

We catch Lady Mary at her most unguarded with her maid, as when she turned to her after discovering Kemal Pamuk has died in her bed. Then there was the time she held her sobs until her mother and sisters had left the room and only Anna remained, after hearing the news that Matthew had become engaged to Lavinia Swire. One wonders whether the feelings are reciprocated. 'She has a close relationship with Lady Mary,' says Froggatt. 'But she understands that her world is not just about material things. Everyone's life has its problems. And the problems faced by Lady Mary and the family can be huge. Worrying about preserving the house, the way of life, the traditions. She prefers the world that she knows.'

Now that Lady Mary is planning to get married, she wants Anna formally appointed as her own lady's maid, but Mrs Hughes is unable to replace her as head housemaid quickly enough to release her. For now, Anna must juggle her duties, which is not an easy thing for her to do. Hierarchy permeates every part of Downton Abbey, and the housemaids are not excepted. As one junior maid of the early twentieth century recalled: 'Wherever we went about the house together, such as to meals or to do the lunch and dinnertime tidying, the housemaids – Alice, Emma and myself – walked in single file; as we approached a door, I had to walk forward, open it, and stand aside while they passed through.'

The same divisions were applied to the housework. As a maid in another establishment described it: 'We each had our allotted task [when tidying the drawing room while the family were having lunch]. In this house with three housemaids, Annie, the head, would straighten the newspapers and magazines … Florence, the second housemaid, shook up the cushions and emptied the ashtrays. I, being the third, swept the ashes into a pile under the grate, and folded the towels and cleaned the washbasin in the cloakroom.' When cleaning the rooms in the morning, before the family had got up, the head housemaid was expected to undertake all the delicate tasks herself – dusting the most valuable objects and the finest pieces of furniture. In the new era of labour-saving devices, the head housemaid would be put in charge of these, too – not that Anna is terribly excited by them.

Awaiting her formal promotion, Anna must remain as head housemaid, and therefore in uniform. At least for this series she, and the other maids, have new uniforms for the first time since the beginning of the programme. This was done to give them a more contemporary look. For their black evening dresses, the hemlines are up and off the ankle for 1920, the skirt is narrower, and instead of puffed sleeves and a high neck, there is a collar. Their day dress, which they wear to do the cleaning in, is a more modern print, although in the same green as before, and there is a double-breasted button detail on the plastron (the front breast panel). The maids wear rather prettier T-bar shoes instead of ankle boots. Everything has a simpler finish to it and the head frills have moved forward.

For all the hard work of a head housemaid, it may be that there are elements of her career advancement Anna is happy to leave for the moment, as there will be many new responsibilities to take on when she becomes a lady's maid proper. For example, if Anna were to join Lady Mary on trips or overnight visits she would be expected to oversee many of the practicalities of the journey, starting with the packing. As one lady's maid recalled, this was a process fraught with trouble: 'Choosing what to take wasn't easy. Mistresses before they leave are apt to be a bit hasty and short with you with their "Oh, the usual things, you know what I like," or "I'll leave it to you, Rose," but when you get to the other end and you haven't brought what they want it's a very different story, and you are to blame. I soon learnt to be relentless in my questions of them.'

Choosing what to pack was one thing; ironing and folding it all, quite another. A lady's maid would take primary charge of her mistress's finest clothes, petticoats and underclothes, all of which required hand-washing, delicate mending and ironing. Up until the First World War, ironing was done with heavy,

solid, cast-iron irons, which had to be heated up on the stove. They often picked up smuts while they were being heated, didn't stay hot for long and were consequently far from constant in temperature as they ironed. As one long-suffering maid recalled: 'Either the iron was too hot, which caused a brown mark called a burn, or else it was too cold which caused a brown mark called iron mould, and well-meant efforts to remove either by dipping them in blue water merely turned the material pea green. It was a heartbreaking, back-breaking business.'

Once the luggage was packed, it was the lady's maid who had to get her mistress's trunks safely stowed onto the train or ship. Successful maids soon learnt that they were much aided in this if they handsomely tipped a guard or porter; then they, the cases and hat boxes would be well looked after. When boarding a train it was important not only to secure a good first-class compartment for your mistress but also to make sure that there was a good third-class compartment close by for yourself.

Edith Bates is older than you and you're as happy as lovebirds.

Anna Well, our situation is hardly ideal, but yes, we're very happy together.

Edith Which is all that matters. As I keep telling them.

With her husband in prison, the question of being married while in service is not raised for the moment. As Lord Grantham is so fond of both Anna and Bates, there will be no difficulty for them if they are united again under his roof (he has promised them a cottage on the estate). But in many large households, romantic relationships between the staff were frowned upon. This was partly a matter of morals, an area usually presided over by a straight-backed housekeeper and butler. Despite the best efforts to keep the sexes separate, 'a lot went on' between young footmen and housemaids. One butler warned all the young males under his care against ruining their futures 'for the sake of five minutes' excitement'. And it was worse for the maids: if they became

Bates and Anna's relationship
has been tested time and time
again, but their relationship
strengthens with every challenge.

pregnant they were dismissed. But even stable relationships were not always welcomed. In some houses they, too, were a sackable offence. Sir Colin and Lady Keppel's housemaid, stepping out with the butler, had to make sure they were never seen arriving back at the house together – he would stay in the village to have a drink, returning later. Nevertheless, many marriages did take place between servants in these large households. It could scarcely be otherwise. As one Lancashire butler said, 'You mostly married domestics; they were the only ones you ever met. Butlers always married a housemaid or a kitchen maid, or a lady's maid sometimes.'

For a woman servant, marriage often meant the end of her life in service – but not always. It was only with the arrival of children that it became inevitable. With Bates behind bars, this does not look likely for Anna for quite some time. It will be a cause of sadness – one of Anna's happiest moments was when Bates was telling her of his plans to get them a country house hotel, so that they could raise their children around them while they worked together. Until he is released, her own future is as bleak, as shut up behind steel doors, as that of her husband. Despite the many obstructions they have so far overcome to be together, this is the hardest one of all and depends on her alone to thwart it. But, surely, if anyone can do it, Anna can.

As a lady's maid, Anna would have kept abreast of the latest fashions in dress and hairstyles. Although the new 'Marcel wave' was supposed to be a simple, low-maintenance hairstyle, it took considerable practice to get it right. Many lady's maids practised on themselves.

MRS REGINALD CRAWLEY

MOTHER OF
MATTHEW CRAWLEY ESQ.

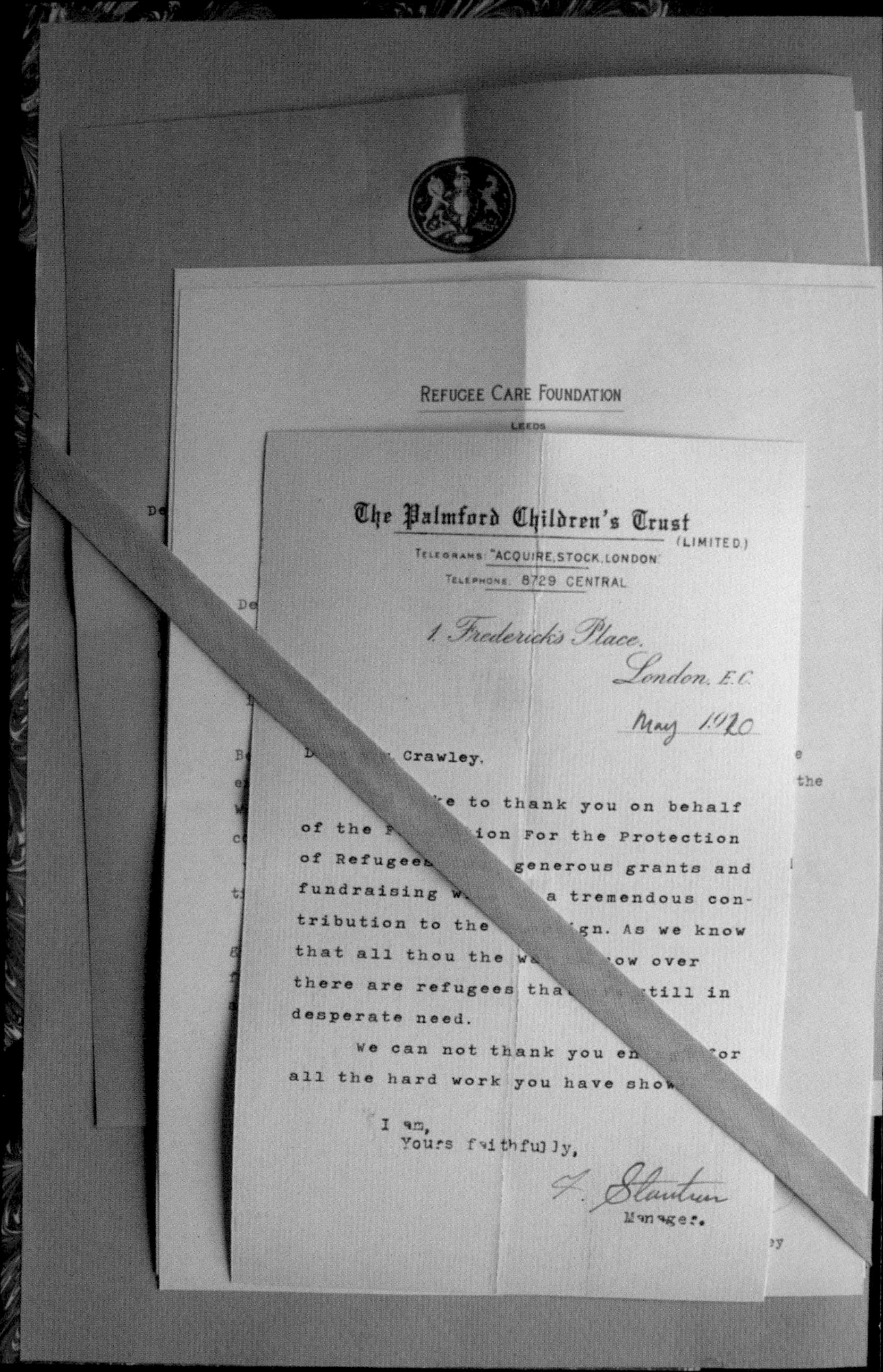

The very limited social welfare provided by the state in 1920 – and the capability of many newly emancipated upper- and middle-class women – persuaded women like Isobel Crawley to throw themselves into charitable work. One such initiative was the Personal Service Association, founded by Lady Salisbury, Margot Asquith and others, for those women who wanted to give time rather than money to schemes of social improvement.

REFUGEE CARE FOUNDATION

LEEDS

The Palmford Children's Trust
(LIMITED.)

TELEGRAMS "ACQUIRE, STOCK, LONDON"

TELEPHONE 8729 CENTRAL

1 Frederick's Place,

London, E.C.

May 1920

D   Crawley,

      ke to thank you on behalf
of the F   ion For the Protection
of Refugee   generous grants and
fundraising w   a tremendous contribution to the   ign. As we know
that all thou the w   ow over
there are refugees tha   till in
desperate need.

      We can not thank you en   for
all the hard work you have sho

      I am,
      Yours faithfully,

      F. Stanton
      Manager.

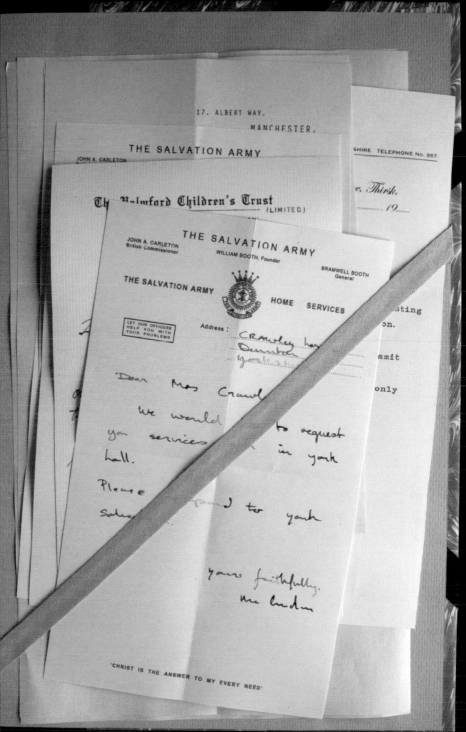

17, ALBERT WAY,

MANCHESTER.

THE SALVATION ARMY

JOHN A. CARLETON

SHIRE TELEPHONE NO. 957.

e, Thirsk.

.... 19......

The Rumford Children's Trust
(LIMITED.)

THE SALVATION ARMY

JOHN A. CARLETON
British Commissioner

WILLIAM BOOTH, Founder

BRAMWELL BOOTH
General

THE SALVATION ARMY

HOME   SERVICES

LET OUR OFFICERS
HELP YOU WITH
YOUR PROBLEMS

Address : Crawley by
Dunstan
York shire

...sting
...on.

...mmit

only

Dear Mrs Crawl...

We would ... to request
you services ... in york
hall.

Please ... ... to york
Solic... ...

Yours faithfully.
Mrs Cordon

'CHRIST IS THE ANSWER TO MY EVERY NEED'

Isobel Well, I don't know this young man aside from 'good morning' and 'good night', but he strikes me as a very interesting addition to the family.

Violet Here we go.

Isobel Crawley is a woman with a cause. The cause may change, but she likes to make sure she's always got one on the go. An educated, forward-thinking woman who lived amongst the professional middle classes of Manchester, she suddenly found herself the mother of an earl-in-waiting. Thrust into this position, she determined that she and Matthew should not be cowed by their new situation. Confident in her own values, she also seized the opportunity to set herself up as the local arbiter of social justice. She was quick to get involved with the teaching hospital, then to work as a nurse during the war (helping Sybil to do the same). She has been searching for a new mission ever since the war ended.

Penelope Wilton, the actress portraying Isobel, explains the subtleties of her character's motives: 'She is not the least resentful – or disapproving – of the Downton world. Though she is critical of the wider society and wants to improve it. But she is not a radical socialist. Her desire to help is conceived within the existing structures of her world.' At the start of the third series, it looks as if Isobel is going to ally herself with Sybil again; she likes the idea of Tom Branson in the family and even suggests going against Robert's orders and sending him the money so that he and Sybil can attend Mary's wedding. Frankly, what Isobel calls do-gooding anybody else would call interfering; even Matthew gets a bit embarrassed, telling his mother to stop starting arguments. When Branson does come to Downton Abbey, but arrives dressed for dinner in an ordinary suit instead of white or black tie, Isobel is deliberately inflammatory.

Isobel sees this situation as another opportunity to challenge Violet's assumptions – the two mothers could hardly be more opposite in upbringing, attitude

and style. Violet does her best to keep herself at a distance, but Isobel never misses an opportunity to tease. As Wilton says, 'There is a mutual respect – as well as a certain amount of amusement.' The truth is that Isobel, for all her confidence that she is in the right, never feels completely at ease at Downton Abbey.

She's not even sure that she likes Mary terribly much, although she will admit that her son is at his happiest with her. Wilton says: 'Isobel may sometimes be sceptical, but she greatly admires Mary's strengths and her strong beliefs. They may not be her beliefs, but she is realistic – she realises that some things can't be changed.' In fact, it's really down to Isobel that the two of them are getting married at last.

The reality is that, as preoccupied by her causes as she can be, Isobel loves her son very much and his happiness is paramount. They are close, and since his father, a doctor, died many years ago, they have only had each other to turn to. When Matthew discovered that his whole life was about to be turned upside down, it was Isobel who helped him cope with the change. It must have been a challenge for her – having brought her son up as a liberal, educated young man with a bright future as a lawyer, she now had to school him in the ways of his aristocratic cousins and advise him to behave as an earl-to-be should. Yet all the while she was determined that neither of them should forget their principles.

Strallan I wish you'd let me sit in the front.

Isobel No, I prefer it. I've ridden in the front seat many times.

Violet Aren't you a wild thing.

The series' costume designer was keen to show Isobel's fresh approach to life through her dress. 'I love dressing her – she is something a bit different,' says Caroline McCall. 'She is the most practical of the older women. She has been to France in the war and she is always looking for something to do. But her son will be the Earl and she doesn't want to let the side down, she wants to look as good as the others. Her clothes are quite modern, with suits that can go from one place to another. She always has a jacket and skirt. Part of her new look is that she now wears peg-top skirts. They still have a waist but fold in towards the bottom, and the hemline is slightly above the ankle.' There's a new textile for this era, too, a surprise to us perhaps, as it seems so commonplace as to have been around always – knitwear. 'Isobel has a lovely cardigan that she wears at home,' says McCall. 'Knitwear will become more popular as we move forward.'

Isobel As a matter of fact, I've found myself a new occupation. But I'm afraid Cousin Violet doesn't think it quite appropriate.

Violet Can we talk about it afterwards?

Keen to keep her busy-bodying out of Downton Abbey, Violet and Cora have successfully steered Isobel in another direction, albeit perhaps not one they might have chosen themselves. Her current zeal is taken up with the plight of 'fallen women' – a euphemism then for prostitutes. There was certainly a genuine problem with large numbers of destitute women in 1920. The sexual freedom that was prevalent during the war – all those boys home from the Front for only a few nights – had left great numbers of women pregnant, and many of the resulting children fatherless when the men were killed on their return to the trenches. If they were lucky, some mothers had married their men during their visits, which meant they were entitled to a war widow's pension, but many were not (the illegitimacy rate rose by about 3 per cent). Faced with the double calamity of illegitimacy and the need to raise their children, the options available to these women for earning money were extremely limited.

Contraceptive methods were available and did improve during the war, but they were still unappealing and often too difficult or expensive for the majority to buy. Condoms existed but they were made of a thick, desensitising material and their frequent reuse (after a thorough washing with soap and water) meant holes developed. Dutch caps, or diaphragms, were also obtainable but, according to one disillusioned user, were 'thick rubber things made from something like car tyres'. Nevertheless, these methods may have been a contributing factor to the 75,000 'street walkers' said to be working in Britain in 1919. Abortion, too, started to be more widely practised, although these operations were highly

illegal and dangerous: the richer young women would go to 'nursing homes in France' on the pretext of nervous exhaustion.

Isobel Have you come for our help?
You're very welcome if you have …
Wait a minute, I know you, you were
the maid who brought your child into
the dining room at Downton that time?

Illegitimacy at that time was enough to make someone a total social outcast. Madge Gow, a Leicestershire housemaid in the 1920s, was frequently set back by her background: 'I always remember going for a job at Stoneygate and they wanted my mother's name, my father's name and my name. And unfortunately I was illegitimate and she wouldn't entertain me. "Who's your father?", "I don't know." Well, that was out immediately. They always wanted to know all your history, what father did, what mother did before she got married, where you came from.'

Ethel Mrs Hughes said we all have
lives to lead, but that isn't true.
I've got no life. I exist, but barely.

Hoping to receive some help from Isobel's charitable work is the former Downton Abbey housemaid, the unfortunate Ethel Parks, who is now facing a life of hardship, alone with her boy Charlie. With no husband, no war widow's pension and no work as a housemaid, she is at her wits' end. Barely able to feed herself after finding what little she can for her son, she starts to think that perhaps she ought to hand him over to the Bryants, his grandparents. The future she can offer Charlie is a paltry one – as a 'bastard' he, too, would face difficulties of his own later on to get work or marry well. Her decision would be a far from unusual thing to do; as the taint of illegitimacy was so grave, many single mothers gave their babies up for adoption. Frequently, parents would adopt a daughter's child and raise it as their own, and many children grew up believing

Ethel represents the kind of woman Isobel feels she might be able to assist by supporting her in an all-too-common post-war situation.

that their mothers were their older sisters. As there were no legal adoption processes before 1926, this was relatively easy to do; even informal adoption continued well into the 1930s.

'She's very in love with her little boy,' says Amy Nuttall, the actress playing Ethel. 'She wants to do the best for him and initially she thinks that what he needs most is a mother's love. But then she comes to realise that maybe he will be better off with his grandparents, and the stability that they can offer him.' Poor Ethel has gone from being a bright, confident young woman full of hope and ambition for her future, to one who is forced to scrabble for what tiny scraps of work or food she can find. 'She's a coper,' says Nuttall. 'She has a steely side and an essential optimism – even in her position. She is still shunned by society. She hates it. But she accepts that it is a consequence of what she had done. She doesn't rage at the injustice of it.'

In the same way that Isobel would consider herself an optimistic realist, in that she only seeks change within the existing structures of society, Ethel, too, believes that the fundamentals of the world and how it is organised are immutable. Of course, they are both wrong. The world in 1920 was on the brink of extraordinary social change; the effects of the war had acted as a catalyst for a number of developments – from medical improvements and technological advances to the breakdown of class barriers and women's suffrage – that were now going to take a foothold.

That said, some of the feared or promised changes never actually happened: illegitimacy continued to carry with it a social stigma until the late 1960s. The old way of life on the big country estates largely survived until the outbreak of the Second World War. Women's fight for equality did not begin to be won until the 1970s. The aristocracy and socialists alike believed with some fervour that the revolution would come at some point during the 1920s. It still hasn't.

The turmoil of the First World War provoked movements of people across Europe and the Near East, as the old Austro-Hungarian and Ottoman empires broke up. Some of these displaced people arrived in Britain needing support and care. (Agatha Christie based her detective Hercule Poirot on a Belgian refugee she met in England.) Although state provision of social welfare in areas such as health, housing and education continued to grow in the years after the war, there was still a strong belief that voluntary action was an essential component of a good society and should be encouraged rather than superceded by the state. Isobel Crawley was one of many newly enfranchised women active in providing this service.

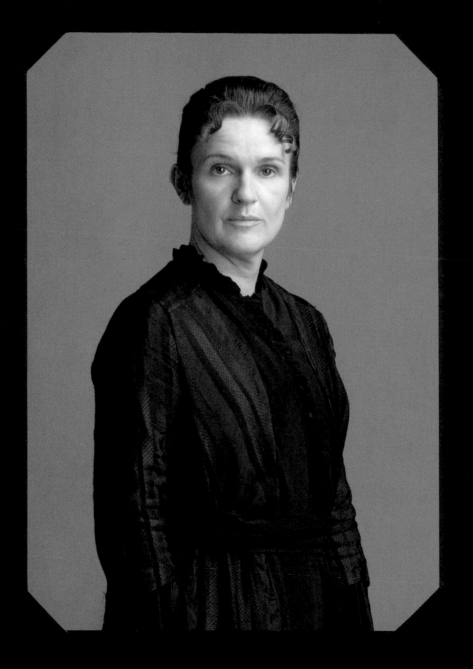

MISS SARAH O'BRIEN

LADY'S MAID TO THE
COUNTESS OF GRANTHAM

As lady's maid, O'Brien would be responsible for looking after her mistress's wardrobe. In addition to cleaning and pressing her clothes, she would be required to darn and mend them and do fine needlework. As clothing budgets were slashed amongst the aristocracy, the lady's maid would also be tasked with updating and altering dresses into more fashionable styles.

No. 51.

Postage Half-Penny.

1D.

NEEDLEWORK FOR ALL

WITH WHICH IS INCORPORATED "THE NEEDLE"

MAPLE LEAF DESIGN LACE EDGING.

CONTENTS.

Published on the 15th of each Month by

THE LONDON GUILD OF NEEDLEWORK,
5 NEWGATE STREET,   LONDON, E.C.

Molesley I'm essential to Mrs Crawley.
She relies on me. That's what he said.
Essential.

O'Brien Oh yes. We're all essential.
Until we get sacked.

S arah O'Brien, an upper servant in an earl's household, would have been considered a woman of position amongst her class in the early twentieth century. Having risen to such a high rank, she ought to be happy, but she's not. Tetchy when spoken to by anyone but her mistress, Lady Grantham, O'Brien refuses to become a part of the servant family, walking alone in the shadows above and below stairs. As Gareth Neame, executive producer, remarks, 'Downton Abbey is a world where people don't say quite what they mean. There is always a subtext.'

There is no one at Downton Abbey that you could confidently say was O'Brien's friend. Even Thomas is less a chum than an ally in her scheming. As valet to Lord Grantham, Thomas is useful to O'Brien as a means of gaining intimate knowledge of their paymasters and the other servants – knowledge that she can use to manipulate those about her. But Thomas is wary of feeding her the information that she wants: he certainly has the measure of her. Rather like two schoolchildren who egg each other on, the pair of them occasionally shock each other with just how far they can go in their machinations. When Bates is found guilty of murder, at the end of Series 2, Thomas's first remark is that Lord Grantham will need a new valet. 'I don't often feel selfless,' says O'Brien. 'But when I listen to you, I do.'

The truth is that they are both as hard and soft as each other, but they express these opposing sensitivities in different ways and they decide who sees these sides of their personalities. Thomas has buried his heart, but O'Brien's bitterness disguises a fierce loyalty that she bears to a chosen few. Her family,

of which we hear only a very little, is among this select group. She successfully persuades Lady Grantham to hire her nephew, Alfred Nugent, as footman behind Carson's back (much to his fury, but she couldn't care less about that). 'As the son of her sister, it is likely that the family has a service background,' says Julian Fellowes. With Alfred to look after, O'Brien shifts her attentions from Thomas, who predictably sulks about this. As he rightly points out, it is not so much who she cares for that decides the question of her loyalty, it is who she can control. When Thomas was younger and greener, he was more easily influenced.

No sooner has O'Brien landed her nephew a plum job as footman than she contrives to get him promoted as valet for Matthew. Thomas is outraged by this, after all he has been through to achieve the same position under Lord Grantham. So we are treated to seeing two former thick-as-thieves friends plot against each other. They are well matched but O'Brien has the upper hand, as Thomas cannot muster a quick enough riposte to her put-downs, which have a streak of black humour to them.

O'Brien Listen to yourself. You sound like Tom Mix in a Wild West picture show. Stop warning me and go and lay out his lordship's pyjamas.

Whether alongside friend, foe or family, O'Brien is set apart from her colleagues below stairs, not only in character but also professionally. She reports to Lady Grantham and no one else – even Mrs Hughes cannot tell O'Brien to do anything, only ask her. Her aloofness would not have been exceptional; ladies' maids enjoyed something of a difficult reputation. Consequently, it was recognised that care had to be taken when engaging them. One butler recorded a list of the questions that should be put to prospective candidates. As well as the usual concerns as to mending skills, tidiness and packing ability, there were inquiries on temper, discretion and reliability.

Even after careful screening, some ladies' maids could be troublesome. One visitor to Sudeley Castle in the 1920s recalled that the lady's maid there was 'easily the most hated servant of all … and this was so in most big houses'. The records of country-house life between the wars frequently echo with the same tale. The renowned socialite Lady Dashwood told how, at West Wycombe Park, 'There were a great many storms, it was always very troublesome … and very often it was the lady's maid who caused the problem.' At Knepp Castle, Lady Burrell wrung her hands over 'terrible fights' between the cook and the lady's maid.

Their position was a territorial one, which perhaps accounts for the defensiveness and troublemaking amongst the other members of the household. Their domain was chiefly their lady's bedroom; only the lady's maid was permitted to touch her mistress's dressing table, and so they became the jealous keepers of a woman's most intimate secrets – from the potions she applied to keep herself looking young to her concerns about her husband. It was an enormously privileged position, but there was only so much that a lady's maid could do with all this powerful knowledge.

Siobhan Finneran, the actress playing O'Brien, explains her character's isolation: 'She has always worked tirelessly hard. She has sacrificed her own life for her job. And eventually she has come to resent it.'

Perhaps she begrudges her life in service, but she doesn't seem keen to alter the status quo. She bristled defensively when Ethel talked about wanting 'the best' and to be 'more than just a servant'. But as much as she may feel aggrieved, O'Brien clearly lives by the maxim 'better the devil you know'. It is the idea of change that upsets her the most – even when it is for the better. When Anna and Mr Bates announce their intention to get married, her reaction is mean-spirited.

O'Brien I hope it doesn't break us up. Having you two set apart in a home of your own, all special. While the rest of us muddle on for ourselves.

Anna You sound as if you're jealous.

O'Brien Oh, I'm not jealous. I just don't want it to spoil things.

What's more, O'Brien is unafraid to make unpopular remarks or stir trouble where she can, even going so far as to write to Bates's ex-wife, Vera, to let her know that he was back at Downton Abbey and with Anna. Of course, she later has cause to regret this when Mrs Bates threatens to expose the scandal of Lady Mary and the death of Kemal Pamuk, which would have caused O'Brien's (now) beloved Lady Grantham untold distress.

It is O'Brien's feelings for Lady Grantham that are the most compelling and extraordinary aspect of her character. When O'Brien suspects that Lady Grantham may be dismissing her, the affront to her loyalty fuels a rage so intense that it leads her nearly to kill her mistress.

Afterwards, O'Brien is filled with remorse and regret. As forcefully as she hated her mistress, she now loves and protects her. It is still madness, but it is turned in on itself. She informs against anyone whom she believes does not have Lady Grantham's best interests at heart – whether it's Isobel Crawley sending Lady Sybil off to learn nursing or Mrs Patmore taking food from the kitchens to feed the jobless soldiers.

The servants are always on their guard with O'Brien, but they don't dislike her completely. After all, some have known her for a very long time, and that kind of familiarity can engender a sort of tolerance. When she is nursing Cora through her terrible bout of Spanish 'Flu, Mrs Patmore is amazed at O'Brien's constant care. 'You never know people, do you?' says the cook of her colleague. 'You can work with them for 20 years but you don't know them at all.'

At no time does O'Brien have patience for innocence and so she is particularly sharp to poor, naive Daisy when she makes unworldly remarks. On hearing that the young kitchen maid is shocked to discover that Lady Grantham might die, O'Brien retorts: 'What do you think happens with a fatal illness? The fairies come?'

While a lady's maid did not suffer a physically onerous workload, her hours were long and irregular, as she was on call for her mistress from the moment she woke until she finally retired to bed. Her principal concern was the appearance of her charge and making sure every detail of her dress was perfectly presented, from the finely darned silk stockings to the jewelled choker she clasped at the back of her lady's neck.

Simply managing the wardrobe was a delicate business, not to mention a time-consuming one. A lady's maid was responsible for all the 'fine washing' and 'fine mending' of her mistress's underclothes and more delicate stuffs. There was also a great deal of 'fine ironing' to be done. Loelia, Duchess of

Westminster, once remarked that 'In those days, of course, dresses were infinitely more elaborate and none were creaseproof, so they never stopped having to be ironed.' Besides which, she said, 'Ladies were completely dependent on their maids – and a friend of my mother's went to bed in her tiara because she could not get it off by herself.'

During the day, a lady's maid would be almost ceaselessly laying out clothes for her mistress to change into and picking up those that had been discarded. Even the removed clothes had to be handled in a very particular manner. Millie Milgate, who worked at several large houses in Leicestershire in the 1920s, wrote that when clothes had been folded and put on a chair, they were then laid over with a cover. 'They always had a fancy cover – some were made of silk, some were cotton, some were embroidered, some had lace frills – and you put this fancy cover over their day clothes that they had taken off ... so that no gentleman could see their clothes.'

As well as contending with the several changes of clothes a day – depending on whether her lady was heading out for a walk, taking tea in her room, or dressing for dinner – a lady's maid would also have to anticipate any needs for entertainment (whether sewing or painting), trips to the village, visits to local acquaintances or packing for a journey. As with a valet, a lady's maid would not be given instructions for any of these events, she would be expected to 'know' what was required for each and every occasion.

Cora You're so good to me.
You've always been so good to me.
O'Brien Not always, m'lady.

Above all else, a lady's maid would be a confidante – there to shoulder the brunt of her mistress's temper, concerns, frustrations, worries and sensitivities. She would be prized for her discretion and ability quietly to find a solution for the more minor cares of that day. From the mistress's point of view, when your maid saw you naked as you bathed, helped you dress and brushed your hair each night, it would be hard to conceal your most private feelings for long. This need for trust perhaps explains why the otherwise astute Cora seems to have a blind spot when it comes to O'Brien. But while there may have been trust and dependence, there was no parity. In stark contrast to Cora's pretty

At Christmas and the festive Servants' Ball, even O'Brien allows herself a night off from scheming to enjoy herself.

looks and extravagant dresses, O'Brien is kept deliberately austere and plain in appearance.

A lady's maid may not have had to wear a uniform or livery but she was expected to dress in a sober and modest way. Miss Russell, who attended to Lady Millicent Palmer of Cefn Park in the 1920s, said that while the choice of outfit was hers to make, there could be nothing 'too bright'. She herself wore the simple pairing of 'a little white blouse and a darkish skirt'. A lady's maid to Lady Cranbourne in the 1920s simmered in a state of resentment almost equal to O'Brien's; she remembered that 'A string of pearls or beads was permissible, so was a wrist watch, but other jewellery was frowned on. Make-up was not encouraged: indeed, later I was rebuked for using lipstick. When ladies and their maids were out together, there could never be any mistaking which was which.'

For Finneran, portraying O'Brien presented a unique challenge: 'It's not like anything you do nowadays. As an actor, you have to negate yourself. You have to learn to be an invisible presence, which is, after all, O'Brien's job. It's why she sees and hears everything.'

Negated, set apart and shadowy, O'Brien is a ghostly figure. It's telling how often she appears suddenly at doorways, having lingered out of sight a little too long, to overhear a conversation that doesn't involve her. There is sparse life to call her own and one wonders, almost sadly, what the years ahead can hold for her. So long as she has Lady Grantham's loyalty, she has work and therefore somewhere to live and food to eat. But if she did anything to forego her employment, her existence would be harsh and empty indeed. With such a fragile future ahead of her, O'Brien needs to find ways to strengthen it, and it may be this that mellows her. One can only hope.

O'Brien, as a lady's maid, was responsible for all the 'fine cleaning' of her mistress's garments and underwear. Much of this would be hand-washed, but some elaborate outfits might be sent to specialist cleaners. Dry-cleaning techniques were advancing with the development, just before the First World War, of very effective chlorinated solvents. (They replaced the highly flammable, unstable and harsh petroleum-based products.)

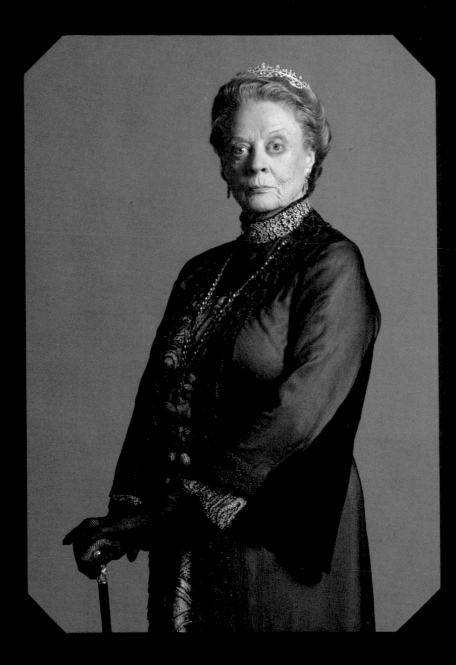

THE DOWAGER COUNTESS
OF GRANTHAM

TABLE OF POINTS   AUCTION BRIDGE

BRIDGE Score	♣	♦	♥	♠	NT
Each trick over 6	6	7	8	9	10
3 Honors	30	30	30	30	30
4 Honors	40	40	40	40	40
5 Honors	50	50	50	50	
4 in One Hand	80	80	80	80	80
4 in One Hand 1 in Partner's	90	90	90	90	
5 in One Hand	100	100	100	100	
Little Slam	50	50	50	50	50
Grand Slam	100	100	100	100	100
Game					30
Rubber					250

Each Trick Declarant
Fails to score 50
If Doubled 100
If Redoubled 200
If Doubled For Fulfilling Contract 50
For Each Trick Above Contract 50
Double value of suit for each trick over book.
If Redoubled For Fulfilling Contract 100
For Each Trick Above Contract 100
4 Times value of suit for each trick over book.

We	They	We	They	We	They
		HONORS			
		100	50		
			60		
		50	40		
		30			
200					
90					
40					
	70				
	72				
	13				
		TRICKS			

Although only introduced in 1894, bridge established itself as the fashionable after-dinner card game with remarkable rapidity, replacing whist in the drawing rooms of the British landed classes, which Violet would have also played when she was the Countess at Downton. In 1904 the rules of the game were refined to create 'auction bridge'. (The game in its modern form – 'contract bridge' – was not developed until 1925.)

Bridge

Score

They

Violet No bride wants to look tired at her wedding. It either means she's anxious or been up to no good.

V iolet gets all the best lines. Intransigent, intractable Violet is the definitive dowager. Largely based on Julian Fellowes's own great-aunt, Isie Stephenson, 'in whom there was a mix of severity and a kind heart', Violet represents the last of an era; one of the few remaining Victorians who believed absolutely in the necessity of moral exactitude, the importance of family and the *oblige* of the *noblesse*. One peeress of the time wrote that the fashion for the upper and middle classes was to model themselves on Queen Victoria: 'That is to say, they copied her more superficial characteristics, her dignity and her selfishness.'

In 1920, the world was looking very different from the one Violet and her generation had grown up in, and in which their Queen had reigned. It now featured motor cars in the street and planes in the air, women voting and cross-class marriages. To cope, Violet and her kind stiffened their spines even straighter and quashed as quickly as possible any notion that these absurd novelties would affect the way they themselves went about their business. Certainly, Violet would have taken her cue from the ruling monarchy, George V, and his wife, Queen Mary, who were both seen as stabilising influences after the war. Queen Mary was very conscious of the dignity of the royal family as well as being a great believer in order. She learned early on that in order to fulfil her role successfully, she should hide her emotions behind a very formal façade. This was considered by many to be absolutely the correct thing to do, in fact the only thing to do, in the face of so much tragedy during the war. That said, it was Queen Mary who, alone of all the distinguished figures

gathered in Westminster Abbey for the burial of the 'Unknown Warrior' on 11 November 1920, broke down and wept almost uncontrollably during the singing of the hymn 'God of Our Fathers'.

But while Violet may fancy herself to be the oil that is poured over troubled waters, others don't quite see her that way. Her barbed remarks frequently sting, even if they also contain more than a measure of the truth. Dame Maggie Smith, who inimitably portrays Violet, believes her character is warmer-hearted than she lets on: 'I think she's been imperious from the age of two and I think she's just about got the hang of it now. I also think — at least I like to think — that she's got this façade and underneath she has a heart of pure custard. That's my theory, anyway.'

Violet I'm so looking forward to seeing your mother again. When I'm with her, I am reminded of the virtues of the English.

Matthew But isn't she American?

Violet Exactly.

When Cora's mother, Martha Levinson, comes to stay, it's clear that she is more than a match for Violet. Equally confident in their age, status and belief that their way is the right way, the two could easily quarrel. But Martha is more inclined to tease Violet, whom she sees as regrettably stuck in the old ways. 'History and tradition took Europe into a world war, Violet,' remarks her American opponent. 'Maybe you should try letting go of its hand.' Violet's weakness is exposed, and she knows it. 'She's like a homing pigeon. She finds our underbelly every time,' she says to Edith later, in a rare moment of self-pity.

But this world is hard for Violet. She felt the effects of the war as much as anybody; aside from her own troubles, a great many of her friends suffered the death of someone close to them. For all their privileges, life was not automatically easy for her generation as they lived through wars and the dismantling of their traditions. Julian's great-aunt Isie married a man whose mother was originally a Rowan-Hamilton, one of the grandest families of Ireland, the last to have a right to a private army and who paid a rent for their castle in the form

of a pair of spurs every year. Isie's father-in-law was equally rich, but money was no help when she went to meet her husband off the ship at Southampton during the First World War, only for him to be carried down the gangplank dying, when she had thought he would run down and sweep her into his arms. She took him home and nursed him for several months as he died very slowly. Later, the family fortunes were lost during the Second World War and her only child was killed then, too. 'So it was', says Julian, 'a pretty harsh life.'

By placing herself firmly at the epicentre of life at Downton Abbey, despite the fact that she is no longer the châtelaine, Violet does not win much favour with Cora (not that she cares), but it does allow her to develop strong relationships with her granddaughters. For Violet, family comes first, and she always has her eye on their long-term happiness, as hard as it is sometimes for them to believe. It is in these relationships that we come closer to understanding that Violet is not a blinkered snob: she knows that marriage is long and that the two people in it need to be sympathetic and share a spiritual kinship if they are to have a happy life together. Although Violet does not wish her granddaughter to end up a spinster, she worries about Edith's keenness on the older, lame Sir Anthony Strallan. For Violet, money is no compensation for mere contentment. 'Edith is beginning her life as an old man's drudge,' Violet remarks to Robert. 'I should not have thought a large drawing room much compensation.'

Strallan Edith's the speed fiend.
She likes to go at a terrific lick.
Violet And do you think you'll be able to keep up with her?

Similarly, once Sybil has made the extraordinary leap to be with Tom Branson, Violet's main concern is that there is nothing for the village to gossip about – she sees it as imperative that the world believes he has been fully accepted into the family. But of her granddaughters it is Mary to whom she is closest; the two share something of the same temperament and they are united in their fervent belief that Downton Abbey must continue to stand as a home for the Crawleys.

One of Violet's sworn enemies is the Prime Minister, Lloyd George. His welfare reforms and increasingly heavy taxation were seen as deliberately

targeting landed families and their estates. It was also the fact that the state was increasingly busying itself with matters of social welfare provision. In Violet's world it was the landowner who looked after his servants, tenants and villagers – not the state. We saw this when she tried to protect Mr Mason from losing his only son, the footman William, to the war. One butler then recalled: 'The older generation certainly realised there was a responsibility towards us: you'd looked after them, and in return they looked after you in a different way. Hence the odd man; you've all heard of the village idiot, but there's no reason why he shouldn't work and have an income. They provided employment as it was needed, making a job for the people rather than the other way round.' Lady Hyde Parker said of her own servants: 'When staff retired they were given a cottage, but I don't think most of them wanted to retire. They just did less and less work as they got older.'

Lloyd George's reforms ended this way of life, as the Duke of Richmond and Gordon recalled of the Goodwood 'gang' (a group of superannuated servants who were allowed to stay on – most estates had one): 'You would see them around the house or the park, sweeping up the odd leaf or weeding when they felt like it. They all had their bicycles and they were blissfully happy.' But with the arrival of state-administered old-age pensions, 'The regulation was that you mustn't earn any extra money at all. So that's when it all stopped.'

Other changes were subtler, harder to pin down. The Duchess of Westminster could not find a date for when the 'little social changes' occurred, she revealed in her memoir, *Grace and Favour*. 'Some things obviously disappeared in the 1914 War; ladies taking the air in carriages in the Park, straw put down in the street outside the house of an invalid, whistles blown for taxis ... But when did the London telephone book go into two volumes? When did they start cutting down the height of signposts so that they could be read by motorists rather than by coachmen perched up on boxes? When did the ranks of bath-chairs for hire disappear?'

One thing that remained resolutely unchanged for Violet was her style of dress. This would have been deliberate. For her, an aristocrat's life is about fulfilling a role, and much of this would be done through one's costume – to demonstrate one's place in the ranks. When Branson admits to not owning white or black tie, Violet cannot comprehend why a former chauffeur would not let the world see that he was now married to an earl's daughter, or at least try to fit in with the crowd around him. His politics and views are beyond her reckoning.

Violet At my age, one must ration one's excitement.

The costume designer modelled Violet's style more closely to Queen Alexandra (they would have been close contemporaries) – King George V's mother – than to Queen Mary. She was a woman to whom many of Violet's generation would have looked, to see how she was coping with the post-war world. By and large, her way of coping was, like Violet's, to carry on exactly as before. 'Violet maintains the high neckline of the Edwardian era,' says Caroline McCall of the dowager's dresses. 'She always has a choker around her neck and a to-the-floor hem. There is a weight and texture of decoration about her clothes.' Queen Alexandra's penchant for wearing a choker and maintaining a very high neckline was, apparently, the result of her desire to hide a small scar on her neck, left by a childhood operation. It instituted a distinctive style of dress that proved extremely influential, enduring even beyond her death. Her favoured couturier was the London-based house of Redfern & Sons, on whom she bestowed a Royal Warrant, as did the future Queen Mary.

In some ways, one could almost feel sympathy for Violet. She may not be lonely, but doubtless she feels isolated at times, cast adrift in the modern world where people no longer dress for mourning, where cars rev noisily down the driveway and the young talk of 'weekends' (instead of Saturday-to-Mondays) and elopements. Yet, throughout it all, she keeps her poise. Smith says: 'It's odd for Violet because she obviously was the king of the castle at one point. But I have a feeling she's older and wiser than the rest of them. And I think she's just, "I've been there, done that and got the T-shirt."' No, pity is not what Violet seeks, but admiration and quiet praise – with perhaps a dash of irreverence, too, just to keep the spirits up.

Violet, like all women of her class, used perfume –
or 'scent' as they always called it – sparingly. Aristocratic
women favoured the citrus-based 'Eau de Cologne'
(developed at the beginning of the eighteenth century
by an Italian perfumier in Cologne), or else the essence
of flowers. Heavy musk-scented concoctions were
considered to belong to the more bohemian.

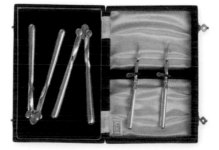

BEHIND THE
SCENES

HUGH BONNEVILLE (THE EARL OF GRANTHAM) EVERYONE ON THE PROGRAMME IS WORKING AT THE TOP OF THEIR GAME – WHICH IS SOMETHING VERY SPECIAL.

The attention to detail on the set of *Downton Abbey* is phenomenal. It infuses every aspect of the production. 'I'm always very moved by the art department,' says Hugh Bonneville, who plays Lord Grantham. 'They strive much harder than any I've ever worked with before to make everything just right. If you are reading a letter in a scene it will be right in every detail – the paper, the handwriting, the date on the letter, the sentiments of the writer. I remember in one scene reading a newspaper at breakfast and they had created a perfect version of *The Times* for that date, so I was reading – in this bald reportage – an account of the murder of the Romanovs. You can't help but feel transported into another place and time, even when there are 30 technicians in jeans standing [just off camera] in the room.'

Talking to the production designers, Donal Woods and Charmian Adams, it becomes clear how subtle, but effective, some of the detailing is. Everything, though, is directed towards telling the story. 'The last series', Adams explains, 'was dominated by great events – the World War, the Spanish 'Flu epidemic. This series is a closer look at the family, seeing them in a changed and changing world.' There is a whole new mood. 'The feeling of encroaching modernity', Woods suggests, 'has always been a key element in the programmes. From the very first scene of Series 1, with its trains, telegraphs and motor cars, it was clear that we were moving on from the worlds of Jane Austen and the Brontës into something that connected with our world.'

That sense of forward movement and connection gathers pace in the third series. In these episodes the design team try to reflect the new, brighter decade.

Between takes locations are alive with activity as the production team primp and preen the actors and the set to make sure every detail is right.

'We are lightening up after the Victorian gloom and the bleakness of the war years,' says Woods. 'We have gone for lighter tones wherever we can.' However, it can only be done in subtle ways. 'One of the difficulties we have', confesses Woods, 'is that in grand country houses they never seemed to buy furniture after the 1880s or 90s.' The main rooms in all the stately homes the location team originally viewed seemed not to have changed at all since the end of the nineteenth century, bar a few modern light-fittings and family photographs. 'At Downton, Robert sees it as his job to keep the house as it is. So it's quite difficult to introduce evidence of the new age. The lightness is subtle in some rooms: Matthew and Mary's living quarters, for instance, are slightly lighter in tone.'

Away from the grand rooms of Downton the post-war world can be suggested more vividly. 'In this series', Adams says, 'there are fewer horses and more motor cars.' And the arrival of Cora's mother, Martha, from America brings what Woods describes as 'a great gust of the modern age'. 'She has a very different energy – from the moment she arrives in a Cadillac, with white-wall tyres!'

CHARMIAN ADAMS (PRODUCTION DESIGNER) YOU READ SOMETHING IN THE SCRIPT – A SINGLE LINE – AND THEN IT TAKES ABOUT 15 PEOPLE TO RECREATE IT!

For the costume designer, Caroline McCall, the new age can be suggested directly through the characters' clothes. 'The constraints of the pre-war world were relaxed after the conflict. This had a massive influence on fashion, particularly women's fashion. Women had a new independence. They were much more active. They could be seen out on their own. They had things to do. In dress, simplicity became key.' The shift from fuss to clean lines has been greatly appreciated by the actresses, who find the clothes much easier to wear.

And this new spirit of feminine independence is picked up, and followed through, by Magi Vaughan, the hair and make-up designer, who researched the period through paintings of the period. 'In the Twenties the women did begin to use rouge, but very discreetly, because they didn't want it to be seen. Hairstyles, too, were changing. They were getting shorter. That is part of the story. The Marcel wave came in from France. And there was the "bob".'

Highclere is just one location used for filming Downton Abbey; in Series 3 the characters are shown in many other places outside the estate, in the changing, fast-paced world of motor cars and new technology.

Highclere, remodelled in 1842 by Sir Charles Barry
(the architect of the Houses of Parliament) for the 3rd Earl
of Carnarvon, is a sumptuous essay in 'Jacobethan' grandeur.
The high-ceilinged rooms are decorated with old masters
and fine pieces of period furniture. As director Brian Percival
enthuses: 'It's such a fabulous canvas on which to work.
It's something that could never be built on a TV budget.'

One of the challenges of filming at Highclere is working
while surrounded by so many valuable antiques and artworks.
Charmian Adams, the production designer, says, 'We continue
to use tablecloths in this series, although historically they
were beginning not to, because the table in the dining room
at Highclere is so valuable. We would have had to make little
coasters to fit under each item of cutlery, each glass, to protect
the surface. But Robert is very conservative so perhaps it makes
good dramatic sense. Also, for filming, a tablecloth is better
because it absorbs more sound.'

The coherence of approach, and the quest for historical accuracy, have contributed to the programme's success. However, from the show's conception, Gareth Neame, executive producer, and Liz Trubridge, producer, decided that if it was going to be a historical piece, it should not feel remote. Trubridge explained: 'The period detail should be right, but it must be matched with lots of energy – and plenty of camera movement.' 'The pace of the stories is very fast,' Neame elaborates: 'It's not a warm-bath of a period drama. We are saying, imagine you are one of these maids, or one of these titled women.'

GARETH NEAME (EXECUTIVE PRODUCER)
ANY CLOSED WORLD DOMINATED BY HIERARCHIES WORKS WELL ON TV. THERE IS THAT ENDLESS FASCINATION OF A WORLD WHERE SOME PEOPLE HAD EVERYTHING AND OTHERS HAD VERY LITTLE, YET THEY ARE ALL THROWN TOGETHER IN A PRESSURE COOKER.

It was an approach that appealed immediately to the director, Brian Percival. As he puts it: 'Costume dramas – for the most part – expect a sort of reverence from the audience towards the material. As a result, they can be rather stuffy. I've always sought to engage the viewer in a visual way.'

Downton Abbey is, of course, a universe of two halves, the grand above-stairs world of the family and the busy below-stairs world of the servants. 'We wanted to differentiate between the two different worlds,' Percival explains, 'the two energies within the same house. Upstairs the mood is serene. To film it we use wider lenses and slower tracking shots. In the servants' quarters we use longer lenses and hand-held cameras. It feels a little bit more real, more naturalistic, almost like a documentary. We *feel* with them. You must be careful not to overdo it – just enough to create the effect, even on a subliminal level.'

Other, more subtle visual tricks are also used to enhance the mood of particular scenes. Nigel Willoughby, the director of photography, is eloquent about the possibilities of new technology: 'With new digital cameras you can change the colour temperature at the touch of a button. It is a whole paint box. As long

The below-stairs scenes are filmed at Ealing Studios on a specially built set. There they can create the darker, more monochrome workplace of the servants without any restrictions.

as you are consistent with each scene, it can be very effective. For example, everything we shot on Bates [in prison] is very cold, very blue. It has its own look, away from the warm world of Downton, and it reflects what prison is like.'

The 'below-stairs' world of Downton Abbey is filmed on a specially constructed set at Ealing Studios in West London, while the 'above-stairs' world is filmed on location at Highclere Castle in Hampshire. The reconstructed below-stairs rooms are arranged in imitation of the servants' quarters at Highclere (which now house modern kitchens and public exhibition spaces). The stairs leading up to the green baize door which opens into the upstairs realm are an exact replica of those at the castle – made out of ingeniously painted wood, rather than stone – to provide a smooth transition between the two worlds.

Working with a set has certain advantages. Individual panels can be removed to allow cameras a clear sight of the action or for 'smoke' to be billowed into the kitchen from concealed apertures. The rooms are all open at the top, their ceilings replaced with a constellation of lights in large, spherical, white paper lanterns. (The whole set is taken down and reassembled between each series.)

The thematic colouring of the servants' quarters extends even beyond Downton itself. 'We've kept that monochrome downstairs palette going in other ways, as it relates to characters from that world. It is there in the look of Mr Bates's house and, of course, in the prison.'

BRIAN PERCIVAL (DIRECTOR) I TRY TO INVITE AUDIENCES INTO THE WORLD OF DOWNTON ABBEY. WE ARE NOT ASKED JUST TO STAND BACK AND OBSERVE; WE ARE ASKED TO BE PART OF IT.

The stairs lead to the green baize door which separates the domains of the family and the staff. In reality, one world is in Ealing and the other at Highclere, but for accuracy the below-stairs rooms on the Ealing set are laid out to echo those at Highclere.

There are different challenges to working on location at Highclere, as a stately home that has a new life as a popular visitor attraction and events venue. The soundman has taped onto his elaborate sound-station, with its banks of monitors, flashing lights and dials, a large handwritten note saying 'FRIDGE'. It is to remind him to switch off the large catering fridge in the nearby modern kitchen during each take, otherwise a resonant 'hum' can be heard in the background. Outside, ingeniously constructed hollow fibreglass pedestals surmounted by urns are used to cover up the conspicuous modern floodlights that surround the house.

One other feature of filming at Highclere is the temperature. Set on rising ground, the house attracts chill winds from every direction. 'It's got its own microclimate,' says Trubridge. 'Even on a hot day it's cold. On a cold day it's freezing.' The pervasive chill lends a curious element to filming. Cora rehearses one scene looking un-countess-like in a floor-length black Puffa coat, with Ugg boots on. Everyone else is similarly swaddled. Even Carson is in a Puffa.

LIZ TRUBRIDGE (PRODUCER) THE FIRST DAY EVER THAT WE SHOT AT HIGHCLERE IT WAS MINUS 6 IN THE COURTYARD. SIOBHAN [O'BRIEN] DROPPED HER CIGARETTE IT WAS SO COLD!

Matters can be exacerbated by the need to film scenes out of sequence. (The production is shot in 'blocks' of two episodes, with the scenes rarely shot in order.) The first day's shooting on Series 3 – in mid-February – was depicting a summer's day. All the cast, dressed in light summer costumes, had hot-water bottles, blankets and coats waiting off camera, to warm them up between takes.

The bedrooms of the Crawley family are now created at Ealing, but constructed to the exact proportions of the Highclere bedrooms. 'That was one of the things we learnt from the first series,' explains Trubridge. 'It proved very difficult to film in the bedrooms at Highclere. They were just too small. It was awkward getting the camera crew in, and it was hard to control the temperature, as you weren't supposed to open the windows. At Ealing it is much easier. The space is altered by set builders – repainted, repapered, re-dressed and refurnished – as it changes, say, from Lady Mary's to Lord Grantham's room. Each transformation takes only a day – a miracle of speed and efficiency!'

While in a grand country house there was a division between the bustling, unseen, below-stairs rooms and the calm grandeur of the family's upstairs quarters, in the world of television the division is between on screen and off. Each deftly crafted scene is framed by a huge amount of work. As Daisy and Mrs Patmore cook in the kitchen or Mary and Matthew flirt in the library, just out of shot there hovers a whole army of costume people, make-up artists, prop providers, scene builders, designers, producers, assistant directors, sound engineers, light riggers, camera operators, cooks and runners – all dedicated to realising the vision of the director and writer and focused on bringing Downton Abbey

Hot-water bottles, thick Puffa coats and any other warm items of clothing are essential kit during rehearsals and in between takes, in order to fend off the freezing temperatures at Highclere.

vividly to life. Some are standing by. Others are actively engaged: the camera, fixed on a dolly, is being rolled along a short length of rail-track by one man. Or, during a kitchen scene, two men are operating a 'smoke' machine, billowing clouds of vapour through a hole at the back of the range. In 'video village' – in front of a bank of small video monitors – the director, producer and DOP (director of photography) sit hunched in their canvas chairs, watching the scene unfold. But between each take this army springs into action. In an instant the set fills with frantic activity; make-up artists leap forward to apply dabs of 'mattifier' (to prevent the actors' faces becoming shiny) or to make minor adjustments. 'The most infuriating thing', Vaughan confides, 'is to have one hair sticking up. We have a stiff bristle brush and can flatten it down with that.' Hugh Bonneville is so tall he has to bend at the waist to have his make-up touched up on set.

JASON GILL (WARDROBE MASTER) THE FOOTMEN'S WHITE GLOVES ARE HARD TO KEEP CLEAN, ESPECIALLY WHEN THEY ARE SERVING RED WINE (GRAPE JUICE).

The costume team take the opportunity to rush in to rearrange the fall of a drape, the turn of a collar. It is a constant battle to keep costumes looking trim – especially for male characters. As Jason Gill, wardrobe master, explains, 'I try to get the boys not to crease things. But it sometimes feels as if the entire universe is conspiring against you. Starched collars can draw blood, but the main concern is keeping make-up off the white collars.' Lights are re-set, sound booms manoeuvred and 'marks' put down on the floor to make sure each actor knows where to stand. Surveying the scene, Jim Carter remarks with Carson-like authority, 'Filming is a bit like life in service – there's a lot of waiting and then moments of frenetic activity.'

As in all productions, there is a mixture of truth and deception; there is much that is real, but as much that is make-believe. As Georgina Melling – a regular extra who appears as a housemaid – admits, 'I thought all the props were fake, but then I had to carry a tea tray. It was really heavy!' The costumes, too, carry the weight of authenticity. 'Stiff collars are a pain in the neck, quite literally,' says Bonneville. 'But they affect your bearing and make you stand in the right way.'

With so much activity and so many people on set, filming is easier if actors know exactly where they should be for each scene. The floor markings are colour-coded to guide each actor into position.

The practicalities of filming, however, require a certain amount of adjustment. Mats are put down on the flagstones to absorb the sound, and the actors also have rubber pads on the soles of their shoes for the same reason. At 6 foot 4 inches, the height of Matt Milne (who plays Alfred) poses certain problems on set. Lucille Sharp, who plays Reed, Martha Levinson's lady's maid, has to stand on a low wooden box alongside him at the kitchen table, so that they can both fit naturally into the same shot.

Working with real food in the kitchen or dining room is a constant challenge. 'Today we were filming with lobsters,' Lesley Nicol, who plays Mrs Patmore, tells me, 'and they were smelly to begin with, and they got a lot smellier. Even a bowl of apples begins to smell over the course of a day's filming.' Occasionally the food is faked (the crew were disappointed to discover that Mary and Matthew's wedding cake was made of cardboard), but mostly it is real. To combat the inevitable problems of things smelling, wilting, melting or collapsing, Lisa Heathcote, the series cook, has devised several ingenious strategies. 'It can take all day to film one scene around the dining-room table, because of the number of different camera shots you need to cover all the characters, so it's important to have things that last. We keep away from cream dishes and, of course, fish.' For the sake of historical accuracy, nevertheless, it is necessary to show a 'fish course' at dinner. 'For this', Heathcote confides, 'we use chicken – or "chicken-fish" as we call it, usually in a sauce. The advantage is, it doesn't smell, and they can even eat it.' When oysters (another dinner-party staple of the time) are called for, cleaned oyster shells are filled with oyster mushrooms.

The food planning has to be meticulous. 'We do menu cards for each meal in the script,' explains Heathcote. 'Things that are relatively simple but look good, and are historically correct.' Another consideration is that, because the diners have to serve themselves, the actors must be able to get the food off the serving platter and onto their own plates with the minimum of fuss. 'We often do things en croute for that reason. Typically, the scene of the family eating in the dining room at Highclere might be filmed three weeks before the one showing Mrs Patmore and Daisy preparing it – downstairs in the kitchen at Ealing. So we have to keep very careful notes – and lots of photos of all the dishes!'

During a day's filming the dishes have to be regularly refreshed, and often the whole meal re-set. For a meal for 18 people, Heathcote has to cook some 70 servings, and in makeshift conditions with limited equipment. 'At Highclere one day,' she recalls, 'I was cooking outside on a trestle table. The plates of

The filming of Matthew and Mary's wedding required as much preparation as a real one, to ensure that not only was everything perfect, but historically accurate, too.

dressed meat were all laid out, when Lady Carnarvon turned up with her dogs, and they all made a dash for the meat. We had to fend them off!'

However, despite the bustle, an underlying sense of calm pervades the set. Michelle Dockery (Mary) thinks this comes from Percival – 'You never see him get irritable' – and Trubridge: 'She is also a big part of it. Laura Carmichael [Edith] says she is like Aslan, the lion in Narnia – a calming presence. We're worried if she's not there!' There is also a great deal of laughter. Lucille Sharp was delighted to discover that 'everyone on the show has such a great sense of humour'. Between takes in the kitchen, Daisy and Mrs Patmore start up a har-monious duet of the Three Degrees classic 'When Will I See You Again?'. The friendships are not constrained by the hierarchies of the characters. As Elizabeth McGovern (Cora) says, 'I certainly don't sit around giving the three girls advice. They do that to me!' 'It's wonderful,' says Carmichael, of the time they spend together at Highclere. 'I just love it – to be part of the gang. Jim Carter [Carson] performs magic tricks at the bar. He made red balls turn into a £10 note! And in the summer we all play croquet.' There is a great deal of professional generos-ity, too. Rob James-Collier (Thomas) reveals, 'It's been a massive learning curve for me. Siobhan Finneran [O'Brien] has been fantastic. Watching her, I saw that it's all done behind the eyes. Otherwise I might have played Thomas like a pantomime villain.'

After three series of working together there is a camaraderie amongst the actors. 'This year it's stronger than ever,' says McGovern. 'We've all bonded with each other.' Everyone who has been a part of the making of this much-loved drama feels touched by the experience of working on, and living in the world of, *Downton Abbey*. As the characters enter the fast-changing world of Series 3, it is clear their story still has a place in the hearts of the cast, crew and viewers alike.

ROB JAMES-COLLIER (THOMAS) THE GREAT THING ABOUT THE ENSEMBLE IS IT'S A WHO'S WHO OF GREAT BRITISH ACTORS.

Amongst all the activity and bustle there is also a lot of waiting around until a set is prepped and ready for filming.

SERIES 3 CAST LIST

Hugh Bonneville — *Robert, Earl of Grantham*

Elizabeth McGovern — *Cora, Countess of Grantham*

Michelle Dockery — *Lady Mary Crawley*

Dan Stevens — *Matthew Crawley*

Laura Carmichael — *Lady Edith Crawley*

Jessica Brown Findlay — *Lady Sybil Crawley*

Maggie Smith — *Violet, Dowager Countess of Grantham*

Shirley MacLaine — *Martha Levinson*

Penelope Wilton — *Isobel Crawley*

Samantha Bond — *Lady Rosamund Painswick*

Allen Leech — *Tom Branson*

Peter Egan — *Marquess of Flintshire*

Phoebe Nicholls — *Marchioness of Flintshire*

Lily James — *Lady Rose MacClare*

Jim Carter — *Charles Carson*

Phyllis Logan — *Elsie Hughes*

Lesley Nicol — *Beryl Patmore*

Brendan Coyle — *John Bates*

Joanne Froggatt — *Anna Bates*

Siobhan Finneran — *Sarah O'Brien*

Rob James-Collier — *Thomas Barrow*

Sophie McShera — *Daisy Mason*

Kevin Doyle — *Alfred Molesley*

Christine Lohr — *May Bird*

Amy Nuttall — *Ethel Parks*

Matt Milne — *Alfred Nugent*

Lucille Sharp — *Reed*

Cara Theobold — *Ivy Stuart*

Ed Speleers — *Jimmy Kent*

David Robb — *Dr Richard Clarkson*

Robert Bathurst — *Sir Anthony Strallan*

Michael Cochrane — *Reverend Travis*

Jonathan Coy — *George Murray*

Kevin R. McNally — *Horace Bryant*

Christine Mackie — *Daphne Bryant*

Douglas Reith — *Lord Merton*

Charlie Anson — *Larry Grey*

Michael Culkin — *Archbishop of York*

Tim Pigott-Smith — *Sir Philip Tapsell*

Charles Edwards — *Michael Gregson*

Bernard Gallagher — *Bill Molesley*

Terence Harvey — *Jarvis*

Ruairi Conaghan — *Kieran Branson*

John Henshaw — *Tufton*

ACKNOWLEDGEMENTS

There are two people without whom this book would not exist, not only because of their professional excellence but because of their enormous generosity towards this project, and our part in it: Julian Fellowes and Gareth Neame. To them, above all, we want to say thank you.

It has been great, too, to know that we were working with a brilliant team at HarperCollins, all of them completely committed to producing the very best book possible. Our thanks to Hannah MacDonald, Helen Wedgewood, Emily Labram, Myfanwy Vernon-Hunt, Jane Beynon, Katherine Patrick and Sally Cole.

A huge helping of thanks, too, to the three Milk (Publicity) maids – Una Maguire, Victoria Brooks and Jessica Morris. Also to our agents Rowan Lawton of Furniss & Lawton, Annabel Merullo of PFD, representing Carnival Films, and Mark Lucas at LAW. Also thanks to Emma Kitchener-Fellowes for her valuable insights and deep knowledge of the period.

The entire cast and crew of *Downton Abbey* have given so generously of their time for this book, even as they were stretched to the limit with their filming schedule. There's no one on the production, actors or crew, who hasn't contributed in some way.

In researching the historical aspects of the book, the London Library has, as ever, been an invaluable resource; thanks to its dedicated staff for all their care and attention.

This book is full of historical detail and a layered knowledge that comes only from years of research and interest – we can only claim a very tiny part of it. For the rest we are deeply indebted to the voices and works of Emma Kitchener-Fellowes, Juliet Nicolson, Virginia Nicholson and the late Loelia Ponsonby, the Duchess of Westminster.

Lastly and far from leastly, from Jessica Fellowes, 'My most loving and grateful thanks to Simon, Beatrix, Louis and George. I'm all yours again … Well, 'til the next one … '

FURTHER READING

Allen, E., *Home Sweet Home: A History of Housework* (1979)

Annual Register 1920 (1921)

Arlen, Michael, *The Green Hat* (Robin Clarke, London, 1924)

Asquith, Margot, *Autobiography* (1920)

Bailey, Catherine, *Black Diamonds* (2007)

Balderson, Eileen, with Goodland, Douglas, *Backstairs Life in a Country House* (1982)

Bapasola, Jeri, *Household Matters: Domestic Service at Blenheim Palace* (2007)

Blythe, Ronald, *The Age of Illusion: England in the Twenties and Thirties, 1919–1940* (1963)

Brassley, Burchardt & Thompson, eds, *The English Countryside Between the Wars* (2006)

Burnett, J., *Useful Toil: Autobiographies of working people from the 1820s to 1920s* (1984)

Cannadine, David, *The Decline and Fall of the British Aristocracy* (Picador, London, 1992)

Cannadine, David, *Class in Britain* (Penguin, London, 2000)

Country Life (1920)

Creasy, J. S. & Ward, S. B., *The countryside between the wars, 1918–1940* (Batsford, London, 1984)

Dean, Charles, 'Boot Boy's Story' in *Gentlemen's Gentlemen: my friends in service,* ed. Rosina Harrison (1976)

Fielding, Daphne, *Emerald and Nancy* (Eyre & Spottiswode, London, 1968)

Forsythe, W. J., *Prison Discipline, Reformatory Projects and the English Prison Commission 1895–1939* (1990)

Foster, Roy, *The Oxford History of Ireland* (Oxford University Press, Oxford, 1992 ed.)

Gorst, Frederick, *Carriages and Kings* (1956)

Graves, Robert & Hodge, Alan, *The Long Weekend – A Social History of Great Britain 1918–39* (1941)

Grimmett, Gordon, 'Lamp Boy's Story' in *Gentlemen's Gentlemen: my friends in service,* ed. Rosina Harrison (1976)

Hall, Michael, ed., *Victorian Country House* (2009)

Hardyment, Christine, *From Mangle to Microwave: The Mechanisation of Household Work* (Polity Press, 1988)

Harrison, Rosina, *Rose, My life in service* (Penguin, London, 1975)

Hattersley, Roy, *Borrowed Time* (Little Brown, London, 2007)

Henderson, Carol & Tovey, Heather, *Searching for Grace* (Steele Roberts Publishers, Wellington, New Zealand, 2010)

Holmes, Michael, *The Country House Described* (1987)

Horn, Pamela, *Life Below Stairs in the Twentieth Century* (2001)

Horn, Pamela, *Women in the 1920s* (1995)

Horne, Eric, *What the Butler Winked at* (1923)

Huggett, F. E., *Life Below Stairs – Domestic Servants in England* (1977)

Huxley, Aldous, *Chrome Yellow*

Illustrated London News (1920)

Inch, Arthur, *Reminiscences* in *Gentlemen's Gentlemen: my friends in service*, ed. Rosina Harrison (1976)

James, John, *The Memoirs of a House Steward* (1949)

Jennings, Charles, *Them and Us: The American Invasion of British High Society* (The History Press, 2007)

Johnson, Paul, *Modern Times* (2006)

King, Ernest, *The Green Baize Door* (1963)

The Lady (1920)

Loelia, Duchess of Westminster, *Grace and Favour* (Weidenfeld & Nicolson, London, 1961)

Looking Back at Britain – decadence and change 1920s (Reader's Digest, 2010)

Masterman, C. F. G., *England After the War* (1922)

Mitford, Nancy, *The Pursuit of Love* (1945), *Love in a Cold Climate* (1949)

Morris, Norval and David Rothman, eds. *The Oxford History of the Prison* (1998)

Mowat, Charles Loch, *Britain Between the Wars: 1918-1940* (Methuen, London, 1956)

Mullins, Samuel, and Gareth Griffiths, eds, *Cap and Apron: An Oral History of Domestic Service in the Shires 1880–1950* (1986)

Musson, Jeremy, *Up and Down Stairs: The History of the Country House Servant* (John Murray, London, 2010)

Nicholson, Virginia, *Singled Out* (Penguin, London, 2007)

Nicolson, Adam, *The Gentry: Stories of the English* (Harper Press, London, 2011)

Nicolson, Juliet, *The Great Silence 1918–1920: Living in the Shadow of the Great War* (John Murray, London, 2009)

Overy, Richard, *The Morbid Age – Britain and the Crisis of Civilization 1919–39* (2009)

Powell, Margaret, *Servants' Hall* (Michael Joseph, London, 1979)

Pugh, Martin, *We Danced All Night: A Social History of Britain Between the Wars* (Bodley Head, London, 2008)

Punch (1920)

Rennie, Jean, *Every Other Sunday: The Autobiography of a Kitchen Maid* (1955)

Sambrook, Pamela, *Keeping Their Place: Domestic Service in the Country House 1700–1920* (2005)

Scriven, Marcus, *Dynasties* (Atlantic Books, London, 2009)

Stevenson, John, *The Penguin Social History of Britain: British Society 1914–45* (Penguin, London, 1990)

Stopes, Marie Carmichael, *Married Love or Love in Marriage* (New York, 1918)

Stopes, Marie Carmichael, *Wise Parenthood* (G. P. Putnam's Sons Ltd, London, 1918)

Sykes, Christopher, *The Big House* (Harper Perennial, London, 2004)

Thomas, Margaret, 'Behind the Green Baize Door' in *The Day Before Yesterday,* ed. Noel Streatfield (1956)

Vanderbilt Balsan, Consuelo, *The Glitter and the Gold* (George Mann, Maidstone, 1973)

Waldemar-Leverton, Mrs, *Servants and their Duties* (1912)

Washington, George, 'The Hall Boy's Story' in *Gentlemen's Gentlemen: my friends in service* ed. Rosina Harrison (1976)

Waterson, Merlin, ed., *Country House Remembered* (1985)

Waugh, Evelyn, *Brideshead Revisited* (1945)

Whetham, E. H., *The Agrarian History of England and Wales 1914–1939, Vol. 8* (Cambridge University Press, 1978)

Wilson, A. N., *After the Victorians* (Hutchinson, London, 2005)

Wodehouse, P. G., *Something Fresh* (1915)

Wodehouse, P. G., *Wonderful Wodehouse 1A Collection* (Random House)

PICTURE CREDITS

THE CHRONICLES OF DOWNTON ABBEY

Text by Jessica Fellowes and Matthew Sturgis © HarperCollins 2012.
All rights reserved. For information, address St. Martin's Press,
175 Fifth Avenue, New York, N.Y. 10010.
www.stmartins.com

A Carnival Films / Masterpiece Co-Production
Downton Abbey scripts © 2009-2012 Carnival Film & Television Ltd
Downton Abbey set photography © 2010–2012 Carnival Film & Television Ltd
Downton Abbey Series 1, 2 and 3 © 2010, 2011 and 2012 Carnival Film & Television Ltd
Downton Abbey® and *Downton*® Carnival Film & Television Ltd
Carnival logo © 2005 Carnival Film & Television Ltd
Masterpiece is a trademark of the WGBH Educational Foundation

Photography by Joss Barratt, Nick Briggs, Giles Keyte and Gary Moyes

Library of Congress Cataloging-in-Publication Data Available Upon Request.

ISBN 978-1-250-02762-7

Printed and bound in China by South China Printing Company.
Originally published in the United Kingdom by Collins, an imprint of HarperCollins *Publishers*

First U.S. Edition: November 2012

10 9 8 7 6 5 4 3 2 1

The image of Mary's tiara featured on p81 is reproduced courtesy of Bentley & Skinner, Piccadilly, London; Grossmith Ltd supplied the perfume bottle on p295; the map artwork on p212–213 was created by Julian Walker.